SECOND EDITION 3
Student's Book

Super Minds

Herbert Puchta · Peter Lewis-Jones · Günter Gerngross

CAMBRIDGE UNIVERSITY PRESS

Map of the Book

Meet the Explorers (pages 4–9)

Vocabulary	Language Focus	Story
Review of Numbers	• Be good at + ing • Possessive Apostrophe	The Old Book **Value** Courage **Phonics** Short Vowel Sounds

▶ Song: The Explorers

1 Our School (pages 10–21) — What kinds of puzzles are there?

Vocabulary	Language Focus	Story	Skills	Think and Learn
School Subjects	• Like / Don't like + ing • Have to + Infinitive	Getting Help **Phonics** Letter Names	• Reading • Reading, Listening, and Speaking **Value** Accepting Others	Math: Geometric Shapes

▶ Song: Lots of Puzzles ▶ Communication: Favorite Subjects ▶ Writing: My Portfolio

2 The Picnic (pages 22–33) — What's good to eat?

Vocabulary	Language Focus	Story	Skills	Think and Learn
Food	• Questions and Answers with *Some* and *Any* • Suggestions	The Golden Apple **Value** Perseverance **Phonics** The Sounds /ɪ/ and /aɪ/	• Listening, Reading, and Speaking • Reading and Writing	Science: Edible Plants

▶ Song: Good Idea ▶ Communication: At the Sandwich Store ▶ Writing: My Favorite Foods

3 Daily Tasks (pages 34–45) — What's it like to work at night?

Vocabulary	Language Focus	Story	Skills	Think and Learn
Daily Tasks	• Telling the Time • Adverbs of Frequency	Cleaning Up **Phonics** The Letter Sounds *v* and *f*	• Reading • Writing, Listening, and Speaking **Value** Being Kind to Others	Social Science: Jobs at Night

▶ Song: Nighttime Flight ▶ Communication: Helping at Home ▶ Writing: My Family

4 Around Town (pages 46–57) — What do we find in towns?

Vocabulary	Language Focus	Story	Skills	Think and Learn
Towns	• Prepositions • *Be going to* + Infinitive of Purpose	Up High **Value** Lateral Thinking **Phonics** The Sounds /ar/ and /r/	• Reading • Listening, Speaking, and Writing	Geography: Tall Buildings

▶ Song: Lost in Town ▶ Communication: Help a Visitor in Your Town ▶ Writing: Messages

5 Under the Ocean (pages 58–69) — What's in the ocean?

Vocabulary	Language focus	Story	Skills	Think and Learn
Ocean Creatures	• Was / Were • Questions and Answers with Was / Were	The Trap **Phonics** The Letter Sounds s and sh	• Reading • Writing, Listening, and Speaking **Value** Being Brave	Environmental Studies: People and the Ocean

▶ Song: The Crocorox ▶ Communication: Where Were We … ? ▶ Writing: Ocean Creatures

6 Gadgets (pages 70–81) — How are gadgets useful?

Vocabulary	Language Focus	Story	Skills	Think and Learn
Technology	• Comparatives • Superlatives	The Cave **Value** Being Resourceful **Phonics** Long Vowel Sounds	• Reading and Speaking • Listening, Speaking, and Writing	History: Cave Paintings

▶ Song: Look at My Gadget ▶ Communication: Go Shopping ▶ Writing: My Gadgets

7 In the Hospital (pages 82–93) — What keeps us healthy?

Vocabulary	Language Focus	Story	Skills	Think and Learn
Health	• Simple Past: Regular Verbs • Simple Past: Irregular Verbs	At the Hospital **Phonics** –ed Endings	• Reading • Reading and Listening **Value** Determination, Never Giving Up	Science: Staying Healthy

▶ Song: An Apple a Day ▶ Communication: At the Doctor's ▶ Writing: Write a Story

8 Around the World (pages 94–105) — What wonders of the world are there?

Vocabulary	Language focus	Story	Skills	Think and Learn
Countries	• Negatives with Simple Past • Questions and Answers with Simple Past	The Final Letters **Value** Showing Interest in Other Cultures **Phonics** The Sounds /i/ and /ɪ/	• Listening and Reading • Speaking, Reading, and Writing	Geography: Wonders of the World

▶ Song: All the Wonders in the World ▶ Communication: What Did We Do on Our Vacations? ▶ Writing: Write About a Country

9 Vacation Plans (pages 106–117) — How are vacations different?

Vocabulary	Language Focus	Story	Skills	Think and Learn
Weather	• Future with be going to + Infinitive • Questions and Answers with be going to + Infinitive	The Treasure **Phonics** The Sound /ɜr/	• Reading • Reading and Listening **Value** Changing Perceptions	History: Vacations in the Past

▶ Song: Happy Vacation ▶ Communication: Vacation Time ▶ Writing: Imagine a Vacation

- **Language Focus:** Pages 118–128   Practice of Creative Thinking, Critical Thinking, and Cognitive Skills

Meet the Explorers

Meet Ben and Lucy – the Explorers. These two friends and their dog, Buster, find lost treasure and give it to museums. Their lives are very exciting. Today they are starting a new adventure. They are in a castle. They are looking for an old book. The book tells the secret of some lost treasure. But they are not the only people looking for the book …

1 🛡 🎧 001 Listen and say the words. Then check with a friend.

1. upstairs
2. twenty-one – fifty
3. downstairs
4. fifty-one – one hundred
5. basement

2 🎧 002 Listen and answer.

1 What do Ben and Lucy want to find?
2 Where are they?
3 Where does Lucy want to go?
4 Where is the basement?

3 Close your book. Play the memory game.

Where's … ?   Upstairs.

4 Review of Numbers; *Upstairs / Downstairs*

1 Look, read, and write *B* (Ben) or *L* (Lucy).

1 Who am I? I'm not good at flying a kite. ____B____
2 I'm good at riding a bike. Am I Ben or Lucy. _____
3 I'm not good at playing the guitar. Who am I? _____
4 I'm very good at snorkeling. Can you guess my name? _____
5 I'm good at climbing trees. What's my name? _____
6 Who am I? I'm really good at doing puzzles. _____

2 Put the words in order. Say the sentences.

1 good   soccer.   I'm   playing   at
2 I   guitar.   playing   not good   at   the   'm

3 ▶ 🎧 003 Watch, listen, and say.

Language Focus

I'm good at climbing trees.   I'm good at playing soccer.
I'm good at catching flies.   Oops! I'm not good at telling lies!

4 Look and make sentences.

Lucy isn't good at painting.

1  Listen and say what Ben and Lucy are good at. Then sing the song.

The Explorers.
Here they come.
Lucy and Ben.
Adventure and fun.

The Explorers.
Here they are.
Ben and Lucy.
Action stars.

She's good at doing puzzles.
She always finds the clues
And reads them very carefully.
They tell her what to do.

The Explorers ...

He's good at riding horses
And swimming in the ocean.
He's an action hero,
Just like you and me.

The Explorers ...

2 Ask and answer.

What are you good at?

I'm good at ...

3 What are you good at? Write a verse.

I'm good at ...
And ...
I'm an action hero,
Just like Ben and Lucy.

1 Look at the family tree and circle the words.

Jack is Nick's *grandfather*.
Julia is Nick's *grandmother*.
Claire and Ted are Nick's *parents*.
Oliver is Jack's *son*.
Claire is Julia's *daughter*.
Nick is Jack's *grandson*.
Penny is Julia's *granddaughter*.
Oliver is Nick's *uncle*.
Lisa is Nick's *aunt*.
Paula and Zoe are Nick's *cousins*.

1 Nick is Penny's *brother / father*.
2 Paula is Zoe's *cousin / sister*.
3 Ted is Penny's *uncle / father*.
4 Lisa is Paula's *mother / sister*.

2 Add the missing *'s* to each sentence. Say the sentences.

1 Tom is Simon father. ('s)
2 Simon is Tom son. ('s)

3   006 Watch, listen, and say.

I'm Greg.

I'm Gina.

Language Focus

This is Greg.   And this is Gina.
He's Gina**'s brother**.   She's Greg**'s sister**.

4 Draw and talk about your family.

Who's this?

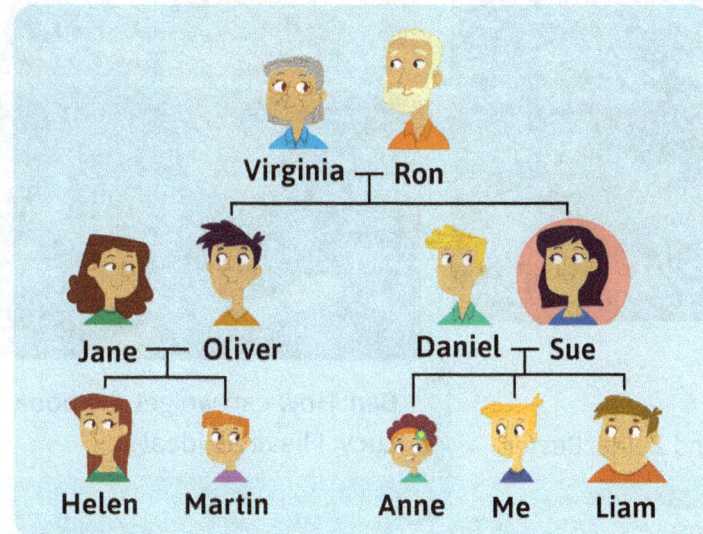

This is Sue. She's Ron's daughter, and she's my mother.

Possessive Apostrophe **7**

The Old Book

1 🎧 007 ▶ Who has the book in each picture?

1
Lucy: What's that?
Ben: I think it's a door. A secret door.
Lucy: Let's open it. Buster, wait here!

2
Ben: Here's the book. It looks really old.
Zelda: They have the book, Horax! Let's get them.
Horax: Wait a minute, Zelda!

3
Ben: I'm so happy we have it!
Horax: Me, too! You're good at finding things that I want!
Ben: Oh, no! Who are they?

4
Horax: Give us the book! Tie Lucy up, Zelda.
Lucy: You can't keep the book. It's ours.
Horax: It's ours now! And all the treasure it brings.

5
Ben: Good dog, Buster!
Lucy: Hurry up, Buster, please.
Ben: Show us the way to Horax and Zelda, Buster.

6
Ben: How can we get the book back?
Lucy: I have an idea!

8 Value: Courage; Reading for Pleasure

Horax: Stop, you two!
Zelda: Go away, silly dog!
Lucy: Stop them, Buster!

Lucy: Run! We have the book.
Ben: Good job, Buster!

2 Write *t* (true) or *f* (false).

1. Ben and Lucy go to the basement. ☐
2. Buster finds the old book. ☐
3. Horax and Zelda are good people. ☐
4. Horax and Zelda want the book. ☐
5. Buster is a dog. ☐
6. Buster helps the Explorers get the book back. ☐

Phonics

3 Find who says ... *Let's get them.*

4 🎧 008 Listen and say.

Gus pats his pets a lot.

Phonics Focus: Short Vowel Sounds

1 Our School

1 🛡️ 🎧 009 Listen and say the words. Then check with a friend.

1. English
2. math
3. geography
4. science
5. IT
6. music
7. art
8. PE
9. history

BIG QUESTION What kinds of puzzles are there?

2 🎧 010 Listen and correct the sentences.

1. Ben's favorite subject is history.
2. Lucy understands the puzzle.
3. Lucy wants to ask their math teacher.
4. Lucy doesn't like the librarian.

3 Ask and answer.

- Do you like history?
- Yes, I do. It's my favorite subject.
- What subjects are you good at?
- Music and art. I'm very good at them.

10 School Subjects; *Before / After*

1 🎧 011 **Listen and write Z (Zoe) or A (Adam).**

1 I love doing number puzzles. ___Z___
2 My sister likes number puzzles. _____
3 I like listening to stories. _____
4 My sister doesn't like writing stories. _____
5 I love singing. _____
6 I don't like listening to music. _____

2 **Where do the words go? Say the sentences.**

1 I love. (singing)
2 I don't like number puzzles. (doing)
3 She doesn't like stories. (writing)
4 She likes to music. (listening)

3 ▶ 🎧 012 **Watch, listen, and say.**

Language Focus

I **like** listen**ing** to music.
I **like** climb**ing** trees.
I **love** sleep**ing** in the sun.
But I **don't like** hear**ing** bees.

He **likes** listen**ing** to music.
He **likes** climb**ing** trees.
He **loves** sleep**ing** in the sun.
But he **doesn't like** hear**ing** bees!

4 **Play the like / don't like game.**

doing number puzzles
listening to stories
singing
doing projects
learning about animals
listening to music
sleeping
writing stories

Do you like drawing?

Yes, I do.

Like / Don't like + ing

1 🎧 013 ▶ Listen and check ☑ the subjects you hear. Then sing the song.

There are lots of puzzles
To find the answers to.
They help us understand
What's false and what's true.

I love learning about the world
In geography.
I love playing sports and games.
It's time to do PE.

I love hearing about the past.
I love history.
Let's turn on our computers now.
It's time to do IT.

I love solving lots of problems,
And math is really cool.
Oh, yeah! I love all the things
That we learn at school!

There are lots of puzzles ...

2 🛡 Solve the puzzles and write the school subjects.

1. h l g e s n i
2. c c n e i s e
3. y t h r s i o
4. h o r p g e y g a

3 Create a puzzle for your friend.

12 Singing for Pleasure

1 Read and draw the missing picture.

Hi Julia,
I know you are in my class this year. Here are some of the things we have to do: We have to wear a school uniform. We have to learn some new words every week. We have to arrive at school at nine o'clock. We have to put our homework on the teacher's desk before class. See you tomorrow!
John

2 Put the words in order. Say the sentences.

1 uniform.   have to   wear   You   a school
2 have to   your homework   put   on the teacher's desk.   You

3  Watch, listen, and say.

Language Focus

You **have to wear** a uniform.
You **have to climb** like me.

You **have to clean** your eyes like this.
You can't? I see. Hehe!

4 Read and play the rules game.

before you go to bed   every day
before you go to school   before you eat

wash your hands

brush your teeth

You have to brush your teeth before you go to bed.

have breakfast

get up

do your homework

Have to + Infinitive 13

Getting Help

1 🎧 016 ▶ Why can't Lucy and Ben read the book?

Lucy: Excuse me. Can you help us, please?
Mr. Williams: Yes, of course. What's the problem?
Ben: We can't read this book. It's in code.

Mr. Williams: Hmm. Let me think. It isn't easy. There are lots of clues in this book. But they're all in code. Very interesting! I like doing puzzles!

Mr. Williams: This is difficult! Can I keep the book? I can tell you tomorrow.
Lucy: Keep the book?
Ben: No, sorry. We can't give it to you.

Mr. Williams: OK then, sorry kids. I can't help you. I have to go.
Lucy: OK, thanks anyway.

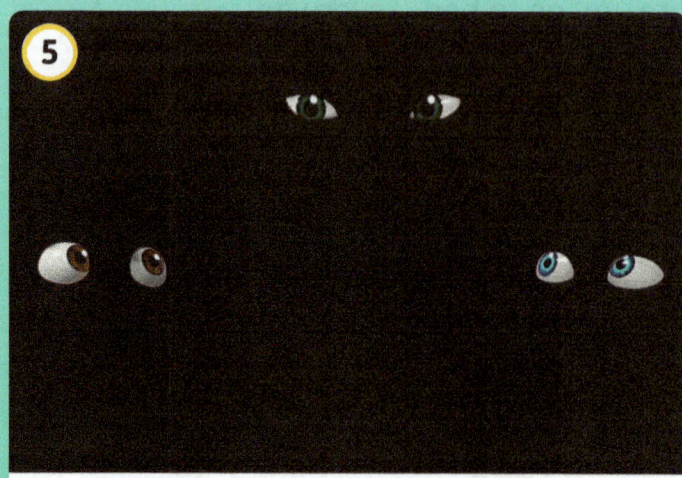

Ben: What's going on? It's dark!
Lucy: Come on, Ben. We have to get out of here.

Ben: Someone wants our book!
Lucy: It's probably Horax and Zelda.
Ben: What? Here in the school? No way!
Lucy: We have to find a way to read this code.

Lucy: Hey, look at this! What's this here?
Ben: Let me see. I think ... Yes, it's the secret to the code. Yes! Now we can read the clues.

Horax: The children have the book.
Zelda: What about the code?
Horax: I don't understand the code, yet. We have to follow those kids.

2 Use the code to write the message from Lucy and Ben's book.

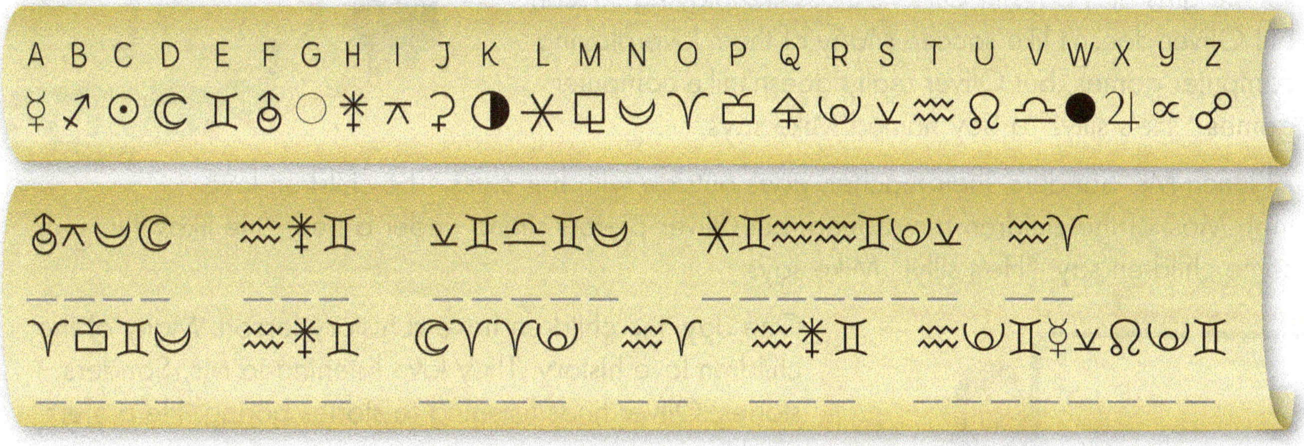

A B C D E F G H I J K L M N O P Q R S T U V W X Y Z

Phonics

3 Find who says ... *OK, thanks anyway.*

4 🎧 017 Listen and say.

DJ **C**ool **K** is on his way from the **U.K.** to the **U.S.A.**

Skills / Storytime

1 Look at the pictures and the title. What do you think the story is about? Write three sentences.

I think the story is about … There is / are …

2 Read the story quickly. Try to find the answers.

1 What is the teacher's name?
2 What doesn't Oliver like?
3 What do the children write down on the paper?

3 🎧 018 Read and listen. Check your answers.

Puzzles Are Great Fun

All the girls and boys in Oliver's class like playing soccer, but Oliver doesn't like soccer. Many of them love playing computer games, but Oliver really doesn't like computer games. "He's silly!" a boy named Mike says.

At lunch Ms. Sanders, their teacher, goes outside with her class. The children love that. Most of the children run around, but Oliver prefers sitting under a tree. "He likes thinking," some children say. "He's silly!" Mike says.

One day, the children have a history lesson. Many of the children love history. They love listening to Ms. Sanders' stories. Oliver finds listening to stories boring. He prefers numbers and dates.

Ms. Sanders sees that Oliver is not listening, and she stops her story. She goes to the board and writes a date on it: August 10, 1992.

"History is full of important dates," Ms. Sanders says. Oliver starts to listen. "And dates are important in our lives, too," Ms. Sanders says. "Look at this date. It's very important to me, but maybe it's not important to you. What do you think it is, Oliver?"

The children are all very quiet now. They are looking at Ms. Sanders, and they are looking at Oliver. "It's a Monday!" Oliver says. "Ha, ha!" laugh the children in the class.

Ms. Sanders tells them to be quiet. "You're right, Oliver! It is a Monday, and it's my birthday. How do you know it's a Monday?"

16 Value: Accepting Others; Reading Skills

"It's easy!" Oliver says. "Write down a date and I can tell you what day of the week it is!"
"That's not true!" Mike says. "You can't know that! You're not a computer. Hahahaha!"

"Take out some paper," Ms. Sanders tells the class. "Write down a day, a month, and a year."
The children put their papers in front of Oliver.
April 10, 2016 – "It's a Sunday!" Oliver says.
September 21, 1999 – "It's a Tuesday!" Oliver says.
January 1, 2001 – "It's a Monday!" Oliver says.
"Now let's look at the computer," says Ms. Sanders. "Mike, come here!"
Mike sits down at the computer. He types the first date: April 10, 2016.
"It is a Sunday!" Mike says. He looks at the next date.
"It is a Tuesday!" Mike says. And when he looks at the next date he says, "It is a Monday!"

"Wow!" the children say. "You're a computer, Oliver!"
Oliver smiles. "I'm not a computer!"
"Can you teach us how to do this?" Mike asks.
"Mm. I have an idea," Oliver says. "Let's start a puzzle club at our school. Puzzles are great fun!"
"Hooray!" the children shout.

4 Put the story in order.

☐ In a history class, Ms. Sanders is telling a story.
☐ Oliver doesn't listen to the story.
☐ Oliver says the day of the week for each date.
☐ Oliver says what day of the week the date is.
☐ Ms. Sanders writes a date on the board.
☐ The children start a puzzle club together.
☐ The children write down some dates on pieces of paper.

5 019 Listen to a summary of the story. Write the three differences.

In the summary we have …

1 ___math___ instead of ___history___ . 3 _____ instead of _____ .

2 _____ instead of _____ .

6 Talk together: What activities or subjects at school are fun for you?

I really like …   *My favorite …*   *I think it's fun to …*

Reading, Listening, and Speaking Skills

Think and Learn

GEOMETRIC SHAPES

▶ What shapes can we see in buildings?

Super Fact!

Triangle shapes are often used in buildings because they are very strong.

1 🎧 020 Listen and point.

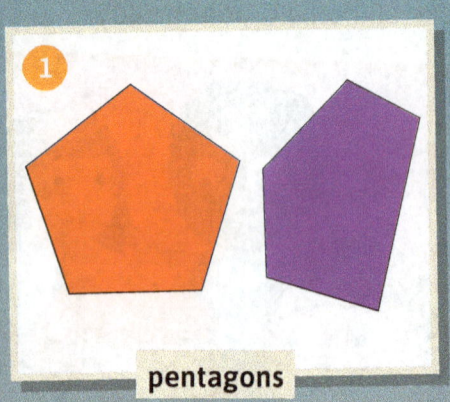
pentagons

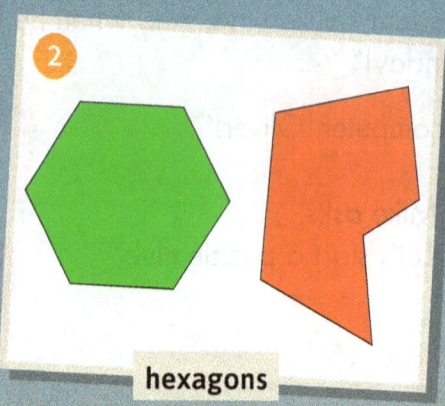
hexagons

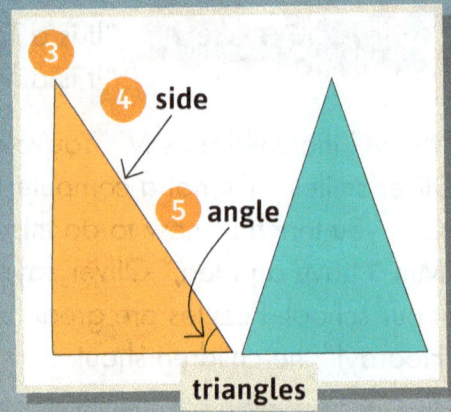
triangles

2 🛡 Look at these sequences. Draw the missing shapes.

1

3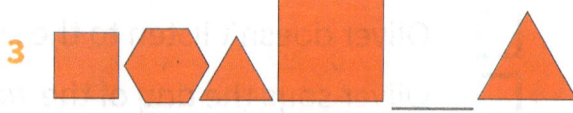

2

4

3 What shape is it? Match the sentences with the shapes.

1 It has five sides and five angles. ☐

2 It has three sides and three angles. ☐

3 It has six sides and six angles. ☐

4 It doesn't have any angles. ☐

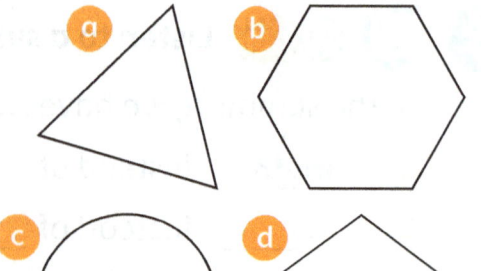

4 **Look at the butterfly puzzle and tell your partner how to color the shapes.**

The kites are blue.

OK. And what color are the small triangles?

5 ⭐ Project Use shapes to draw an insect or a bird. Count the number of shapes, angles, and sides. Tell your friends.

This is my insect. It's a dragonfly. It has six shapes: two hexagons, two squares, two pentagons, three triangles, three circles, and four kites. There are … sides and … angles.

Portfolio

Talk and Find Out

Favorite Subjects

1 Make a prediction.

I predict that my class's favorite school subject is _____.

2 Work in groups of four. Draw a table. Ask and write.

Favorite Subject	Names	
IT	Maria	1
English	Shelley, Joshua, Tom	3

3 Add up all the answers from the groups on the board.

Favorite Subject	Groups	Total
IT	1 + 2	3
English	3 + 1	

4 Make a bar chart and talk about the results.

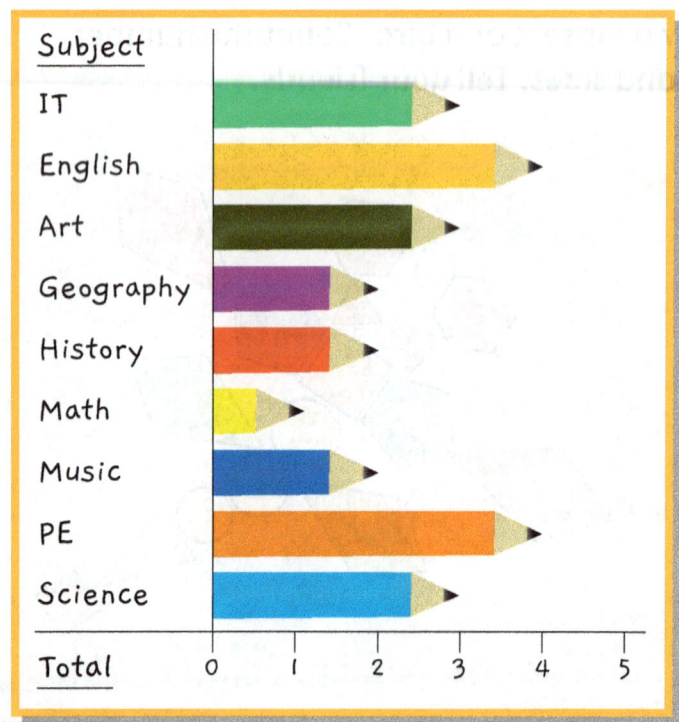

> Was your prediction correct?

> I predicted that my class's favorite school subject was …

> Now I know that my class's favorite school subject is …

Communication

1

Think and Write

My Portfolio

1 Read about the portfolio.

Did You Know ... ?

Your portfolio helps you show your learning progress. You can show:
- your stories and other things you write.
- project reports, bar charts, etc.

You can create a print portfolio or a digital portfolio.

In a print portfolio, you can take photos of your work and stick them into your portfolio.

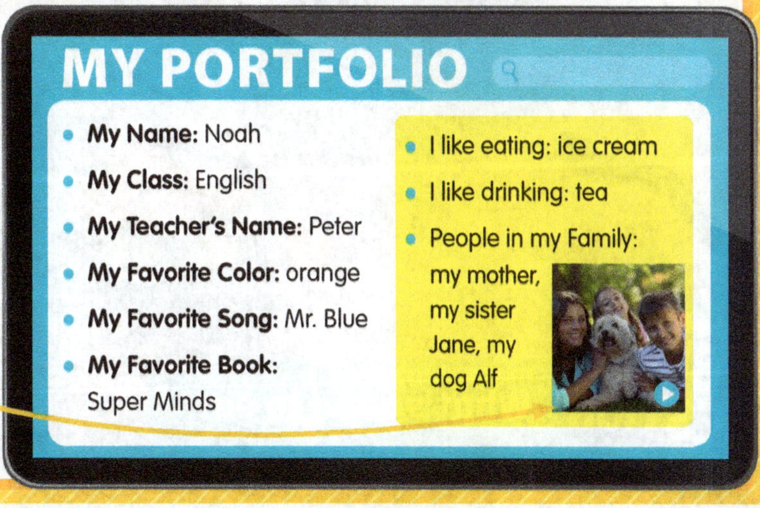

In a digital portfolio, you can upload audio or video recordings of role-play activities and other conversations.

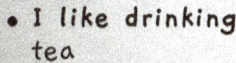

My Portfolio
- My Name: Noah
- My Class: English
- My Teacher's Name: Peter
- My Favorite Color: orange
- My Favorite Song: Mr. Blue
- My Favorite Book: Super Minds
- I like eating: ice cream
- I like drinking: tea
- People in my Family: my mother, my sister Jane, my dog Alf

MY PORTFOLIO
- My Name: Noah
- My Class: English
- My Teacher's Name: Peter
- My Favorite Color: orange
- My Favorite Song: Mr. Blue
- My Favorite Book: Super Minds
- I like eating: ice cream
- I like drinking: tea
- People in my Family: my mother, my sister Jane, my dog Alf

2 Write a profile for your portfolio.

3 Write some rules for your English class.

Writing Tip
Check your sentences for capital letters and periods.

English Class Rules:

We have to speak English.
We have to do our homework.
We have to listen to ...
We have to read a book every ...

Writing

2 The Picnic

1 🎧 021 Listen and say the words. Then check with a friend.

1. apple juice
2. roll
3. cheese
4. water
5. soup
6. vegetables
7. lemonade
8. salad

BIG QUESTION What's good to eat?

Near the town there's a pool. Look down deep where water's cool.

2 🎧 022 Listen and answer.

1. What are Ben and Lucy looking for?
2. What does Lucy drink?
3. What does Ben eat?
4. Why is Buster barking?

3 Ask and answer.

I'm hungry / thirsty.

Would you like some … ?

22 Food

1 🎧 023 Listen and check ✓ the roll.

2 Complete with *some* or *any*. Say the sentences.

1 Are there _____ tomatoes?
2 Yes, there are _____ tomatoes.
3 Is there _____ cheese?
4 No, there isn't _____ cheese.

3 ▶ 🎧 024 Watch, listen, and say.

Language Focus

Is there **any** food in your bag?
Yes, there is **some** food.
Is there **any** cheese in your bag?
No, there isn't **any** cheese.

Are there **any** rolls in your bag?
No, there aren't **any** rolls.
Are there **any** apples in your bag?
Yes, there are **some** apples.

4 Play the imaginary sandwich game.

— Are there any vegetables?
— Yes, there are some vegetables.

Questions and Answers with *Some* and *Any*

1 🎧 025 ▶ **Listen and match the food. Then sing the song.**

1  2  3    a  b  c

Is there any lemonade
In your soup today?
Mix it in, eat it all,
Then go out and play.

**Good idea, good idea!
That sounds good to me!
Good idea, good idea!
I'm so hungry!**

Is there any apple juice
In your salad, too?
Mix it in, eat it all
That's my lunch for you.

Good idea, good idea! ...

Are there any vegetables
In your jelly roll, please?
Mix them in, eat them all
With a piece of cheese.

Good idea, good idea! ...

2 🛡 **What do you think is good? Complete the table.**

	Good	Bad
On a roll	chicken	water
In a salad		
In soup		

3 **Compare with a partner.**

> Chicken is good on a roll.

> Water is bad on a roll.

24 Singing for Pleasure

1 🎧 027 Listen and check ✓ the food in the soup.

☐ ☐ ☐ ☐

☐ ☐ ☐ ☐

2 Put the words in order. Say the sentences.
1 we   Should   in the soup?   some carrots   put
2 And   how   onions?   some   about

3 ▶ 🎧 028 Watch, listen, and say.

Language Focus

It's six o'clock and time to eat!   Or **should we have** some bread with cheese?
How about some peas?   **I'd like** some flies and that's all, please.

4 Make a bowl of soup or a salad with a friend.

Should we put some …
in our … ?

Good idea!

Suggestions 25

The Golden Apple

1 🎧 029 ▶ Why is Buster sick?

Lucy: Buster. Buster, what's the matter?
Ben: Lucy, look, a snake. It bit Buster. Let's take him to the town. It's not far.
Lucy: Let's go now. Come on.

Lucy: Can you help us? A snake bit our dog.
Ben: He's very sick. Do you have any medicine?
Woman: No, but go to the old man in the hut next to the big tree. He can help you.

Man: Take your dog to the top of the mountain. There's a waterfall there. Above it, there's a tree with a golden apple. Your dog has to eat that apple.

Horax: Quick. I want to get to that apple first. We don't want Buster to get better!
Lucy: Look, Ben, there are Horax and Zelda.

Lucy: Look at the tree. It's Horax and Zelda.
Ben: Hey, Horax. Stop!
Zelda: Do you want any help, Horax?
Horax: No. I think have it.

Zelda: Horax, you fool!
Ben: Thanks for the apple, Horax!

26 Value: Perseverance; Reading for Pleasure

Ben: Lucy, look. There's a letter.
Lucy: It's an *I*, Ben. It's our first letter.
Ben: Should we write it in the book?
Lucy: Good idea.

Lucy: Bye, Horax. Bye, Zelda.
Ben: And thanks again for the apple.
Zelda: You kids. Just you wait!

2 Write *t* (true) or *f* (false).

1 Lucy and Ben take Buster to the town. ☐
2 A woman tells Ben and Lucy about the waterfall. ☐
3 The apple tree is under a waterfall. ☐
4 The kids have to find a silver apple. ☐
5 Horax gets to the tree first. ☐
6 Lucy finds the letter in a pool near the waterfall. ☐

Phonics

3 Find who says … *Should we write it in the book?*

4 🎧 030 Listen and say.

I like my little fish and ice cream pie!

Phonic Focus: /ɪ/ and /aɪ/

Skills

1 🎧 031 Listen and answer the questions.

1 What time does lunch start?
At _____ o'clock.

2 Where do the children eat?
In the _____ cafeteria.

3 Which children eat first?
Children with _____.

4 What is Lisa's favorite school lunch?
_____, peas, and French fries.

5 When does Lisa have sandwiches?
On _____.

6 What time does lunch finish?
At _____ o'clock.

2 Read and match. There is one extra plate of food.

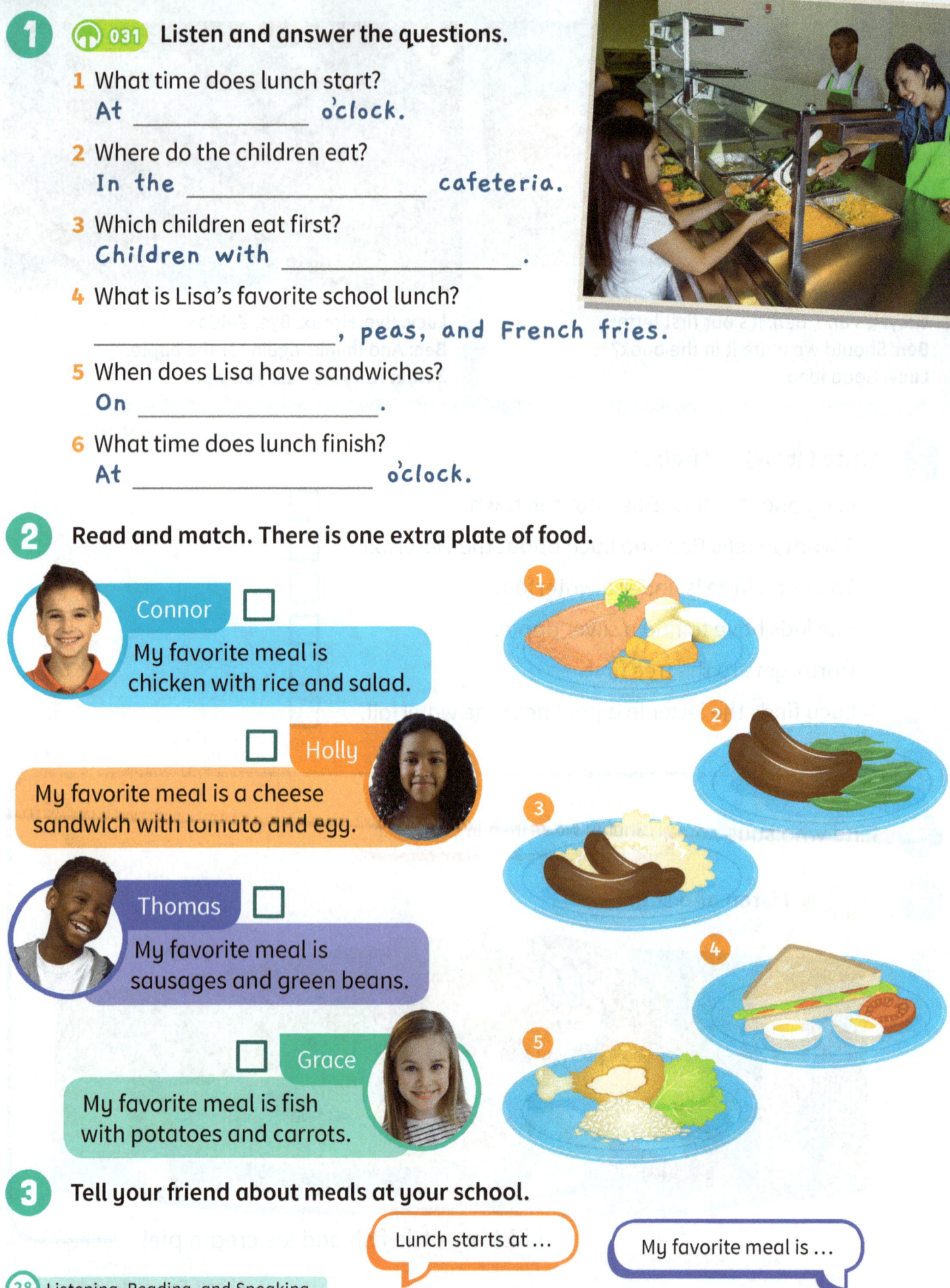

Connor ☐
My favorite meal is chicken with rice and salad.

Holly ☐
My favorite meal is a cheese sandwich with tomato and egg.

Thomas ☐
My favorite meal is sausages and green beans.

Grace ☐
My favorite meal is fish with potatoes and carrots.

3 Tell your friend about meals at your school.

Lunch starts at …

My favorite meal is …

Listening, Reading, and Speaking

1 Read the poem and check ✓ the food the girl eats for each meal.

Breakfast is the meal
At the start of the day.
Sausage, toast, and egg
Then I'm on my way.

Lunch is the meal
In the middle of the day.
A sandwich and some milk
On my school lunch tray.

Dinner is the meal
Near the end of the day.
Chicken, rice, and beans
Then I'm off to play.

	sausage	chicken	toast	sandwich	beans	egg	rice	milk
Breakfast	✓							
Lunch								
Dinner								

2 Complete the poem about you.

Breakfast is the meal
At the start of the day.
_____
Then I'm on my way.

Lunch is the meal
In the middle of the day.
_____
On my school lunch tray.

Dinner is the meal
Near the end of the day.
_____
Then I'm off to play.

Think and Learn

Edible Plants

Super Fact! A tomato is not a vegetable – it's a fruit!

▶ What plant parts are good to eat?

1 🎧 032 Listen and point.

 roots

 stems

 leaves

 seeds

 fruit

2 Read and put checks ✓ in the table.

We make juice from fruit. We can also make delicious fruit desserts.

Asparagus is a stem. It tastes good in soup.

Carrots are roots. They taste good in soups and salads.

Do you like eating leaves? We often eat lettuce leaves in salads.

Sometimes we eat the seeds of plants, like peas. We can eat them with meat or fish.

	Roots	Stems	Leaves	Seeds	Fruit
Asparagus		✓			
Carrot					
Lettuce					
Orange					
Pea					

3 Which food or drink isn't from a plant part?

1 potato   onion   cheese   banana
2 tomato juice water   lemonade   watermelon
3 carrot salad asparagus soup   lettuce   chicken

4 🔊 033 Listen. Match the animals with their food.

5 **Project** Draw a picnic with food and drinks from plant parts. Write sentences about the picnic food.

We make the orange juice from fruit.
We make the salad from leaves and roots.

Science 31

Portfolio

Talk and Find Out

At the Sandwich Store

1 Choose a role card. Read and plan.

The SANDWICH STORE
The **BEST** Sandwiches in Town
Choose any fillings:

- tomato
- cheese
- chicken
- mushrooms
- salad
- carrots
- sausage
- onion

Student A
- You are at a sandwich store.
- Choose three fillings for your sandwich.
- Order a sandwich and a drink.

Student B
- You make sandwiches at a sandwich store.
- Ask the teacher which fillings you have and circle them.
- Find out what your customer wants to eat.

2 Act out your play.

Useful Language

Sandwich Maker
Can I help you?
Sorry, we don't have any …
How about … ?
Here you go.

Customer
I'd like a …, please.
Do you have any … ?
I like … a lot.
Can I have … ?

Communication

Think and Write

My Favorite Foods

1 Think of all the words you know for food and drinks. Write them on pieces of paper.

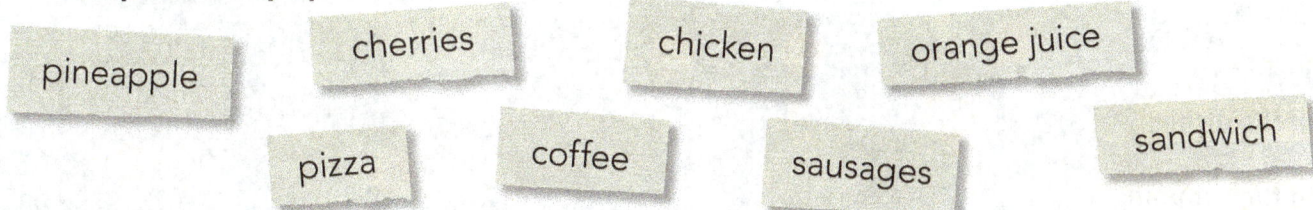

pineapple, cherries, chicken, orange juice, pizza, coffee, sausages, sandwich

2 How many groups can you put your words in? Color each group.

orange juice, coffee | cherries, pineapple | chicken, sausages | pizza, sandwich

3 Write your words in lists.

My favorites 😀	I like 🙂	I don't like 😐	I really don't like 😞
sausages orange juice chicken	cherries	pizza sandwiches	coffee pineapple

4 Write about a meal you would like and a meal you would not like. Add photos or drawings.

> **Writing Tip**
> Remember to use apostrophes for contractions.
> do + not = don't
> I + have = I've

My favorite meal is sausages with French fries and peas, apple juice to drink, and cherries.

I don't like fish with onions and tomatoes. I don't like pineapple and I don't like coffee. Ugh!

3 Daily Tasks

1 🛡 🎧 034 Listen and say the words. Then check with a friend.

1 sweep
2 do the dishes
3 do the shopping
4 clean up
5 cook
6 dry the dishes
7 take the dog for a walk
8 feed the dog

BIG QUESTION What's it like to work at night?

Helping hands, there's work to do. A letter's here. It waits for you.

2 🎧 035 Listen and correct the sentences.

1 The boy calls the dog "Buster."
2 Buster is still feeling sick.
3 Lucy doesn't like cooking.
4 Ben likes doing the dishes.

3 Play the mime game.

Are you drying the dishes?

Yes, I am.

1 🎧 036 **Listen and number.**

2 **Look at Activity 1 again and write** *quarter* **or** *half*. **Say the sentences.**

1  I do my homework at _____ past five.

2  I do the dishes at _____ past six.

3  I take the dog for a walk at _____ to seven.

4 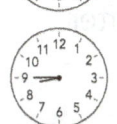 I go to bed at _____ past eight.

3 ▶ 🎧 037 **Watch, listen, and say.**

Language Focus

I get out of bed at **half past** seven.

I get dressed at eight **o'clock**.

I have my breakfast at **quarter past** eight.

I get my bag at **quarter to** nine.

4 **Play the time game.**

It's quarter to one.

That's right.

Telling the Time

1 🎧 038 ▶ Listen and draw the times on the clocks. Then sing the song.

I get up. It's quarter to three.
I get dressed and I have some tea.
I feed my dog. I sweep the floor.
It's nine o'clock, I'm out my door.

**You can only get to the moon at night,
And I'm the pilot of the nighttime flight.
Let's go to the moon!**

I'm in my spaceship. It's half past nine.
I'm the pilot, and I feel fine.
It's half past ten. We're on the moon.
Take some photos. It's time to leave soon.

You can only get to the moon at night ...

I'm now back home. It's half past three.
I walk the dog, then I have my tea.
Wash the dishes – in bed very soon.
Time to sleep and then back to the moon.

You can only get to the moon at night ...

10, 9, 8, 7, 6, 5, 4, 3, 2, 1 ... BLAST OFF!

a

b

c

d

e

2 Read and correct the sentences.

1 The pilot gets up after three o'clock.
2 At quarter past nine, the pilot is in her spaceship.
3 The pilot gets to the moon after eleven o'clock.
4 The pilot never flies at night.

3 Compare with a partner.

get up   leave the house   get home   go to bed

I get up at half past seven.

I don't. I get up at quarter to eight.

36 Singing for Pleasure

1 Read. Put checks ✓ or X's ✗ in the table.

How I Help My Mom and Dad

- I always take the dog for a walk. I do that on Mondays, Tuesdays, Wednesdays, Thursdays, and Fridays after school. I love my dog!
- I usually dry the dishes. I do that on Mondays, Tuesdays, Thursdays, and Fridays.
- I sometimes do the dishes. I do the dishes on Tuesdays and Thursdays. I don't really like doing the dishes!
- I never cook. Never! I want to cook, but Mom says I can't.

by Nick, age 9

	Monday	Tuesday	Wednesday	Thursday	Friday
Walk the dog					
Dry the dishes					
Do the dishes					
Cook					

2 Where do the words go? Say the sentences.

1. I clean up on Saturdays. (always)
2. I help Mom do the dishes. (usually)
3. I take the dog for a walk at 6 o'clock. (sometimes)
4. I go to bed before 8 o'clock. (never)

3 ▶ 🎧 040 Watch, listen, and say.

Language Focus

Gina **always** climbs this beautiful tree.
Greg **usually** climbs the tree with me.

Gina **sometimes** sleeps at the top of the tree.
But Greg **never** sleeps there next to me.

4 Play the true or false game.

Nick sometimes walks his dog after school. True or false?

False. He always walks his dog after school.

Adverbs of Frequency

Cleaning Up

1 🎧 041 ▶ What does Zelda think of the town?

1
Ben: So what does the next clue mean?
Lucy: Well, the letter's in this town. But where?
Ben: Let's look for it tomorrow morning. It's quarter past nine, and I'm tired.

2
Horax: It's here. The next letter is in this town.
Zelda: Let's wait for dark.
Horax: Good idea. We can look for it after dark.

3
Horax: It isn't here.
Zelda: I'm tired, and I don't like this town. It's half past ten. Let's go soon.

4
Ben: Oh, no! What a mess!
Lucy: "Helping hands," remember the clue.
Ben: Yes, maybe this is what we have to do before we find the next letter.

5
Ben: This table is heavy! There's no letter here.

6
Lucy: Why do I always get the horrible jobs? Where is that letter? We have to find it soon!

38 Reading for Pleasure

7

Lucy: What's that? Yes! Ben, come here!
Ben: What is it?
Lucy: I have something to show you.

8

Ben: Wow! It's the next letter.
Lucy: The letter *F*. Now we have our second letter!

2 Answer the questions.

Who …
1 wants to look for the clue in the morning? _____
2 listens to the kids talk about the clue? _____
3 doesn't like the town? _____
4 lifts the table up? _____
5 cleans up the trash? _____
6 finds the next letter? _____

Phonics

3 Find who says … *The letter F. Now we have our second letter!*

4 🎧 042 **Listen and say.**

Vic sells **f**abulous **f**ans **f**rom the back o**f** his **v**an.

Phonics Focus: *v* and *f*

Skills / Storytime

1 Look at the pictures and write *t* (true) or *f* (false).

1. The shoemaker's job is difficult. _____
2. The elves cut leather for the shoes. _____
3. One night, the shoemaker sees six elves. _____
4. The elves make small pants and shirts. _____

2 🎧 043 Read and listen. Check your answers.

The Shoemaker and the Elves

In a country far away there is a shoemaker. His job is not easy. He always gets up at 6 o'clock, and he never goes to bed before 11 o'clock. The shoemaker always cuts the leather, and then he makes the shoes. He works a lot, but he doesn't have a lot of money. One day he cuts the leather for ten pairs of shoes. But he is very tired, so he leaves the leather on the kitchen table and goes to bed.

leather
a pair of shoes
shoemaker

The next morning, the shoemaker gets up and sees ten pairs of beautiful shoes on the kitchen table. He is very happy. That night, before he goes to bed, the shoemaker cuts the leather for twenty pairs of shoes and leaves it on the kitchen table. The next morning there are twenty pairs of beautiful shoes on the table. Every night, he leaves the leather for more pairs of shoes, and every morning there are beautiful shoes on the table!

Value: Being Kind to Others; Reading Skills

elves

Many people in the town want a pair of the shoes, and soon the shoemaker has a lot of money. But who is making the shoes? The shoemaker wants to know. One night he hides under a table and waits. At 12 o'clock the shoemaker sees five elves. They jump onto the table and start making the shoes. The shoemaker sees their clothes, too. They are very old and not very nice. At 5 o'clock in the morning the elves stop and leave the house.

The shoemaker wants to say "thank you" to the elves, so he makes five beautiful small pairs of pants and shirts. That night, he leaves the clothes on the table with the leather. In the morning the clothes are gone, but the leather is still there.

First, the shoemaker is sad. "The elves are not making shoes for me anymore!" he thinks. But then he thinks, "It's great. The elves have beautiful new clothes, and I have a good life now."

3 Complete the sentences with words from the story.

1 The shoemaker gets up …
2 When the shoemaker goes to bed, he is …
3 In the morning, he finds …
4 The next night, he leaves leather …
5 Everyone in town wants …
6 The elves start work at …
7 The shoemaker makes clothes to say …
8 The shoemaker is happy because …

4 044 Listen to a summary of the story. Write the three differences.

In the summary we have …

1 __five__ instead of __ten pairs of shoes__.
2 _____ instead of _____.
3 _____ instead of _____.

5 Ask the elves to help you.

> Elves, please do my homework tonight.

> Elves, please clean my room tonight.

Writing, Listening, and Speaking Skills 41

Think and Learn

JOBS AT *Night*

Super Fact! People feel very tired at 2 o'clock in the morning and 2 o'clock in the afternoon.

▶ What jobs can people do at night?

1 🎧 045 Listen and point.

1. firefighter
2. police officer
3. ambulance driver
4. vet
5. janitor

2 Read and write the jobs in the table.

Job	What They Do at Night
1 _____	These people clean the school.
2 _____	These people take sick people to the hospital.
3 _____	These people stop fires.
4 _____	These people take care of animals.
5 _____	These people help people.

3 🎧 046 Listen and check your answers.

4 What's it like to work at night? Circle your answers. Write one more sentence about working at night.

1. Working at night is fun / difficult.
2. It's easy / not easy to sleep in the day.
3. You see / don't see your family every day.
4. You can do more things / need to sleep in the day.
5. _____

42 Social Science

5 Read Anna's work diary and write times under the pictures.

An Ambulance Driver's Diary

NIGHT

7 o'clock – I eat lunch – My family is finishing dinner. It's dark outside.
10 o'clock – My family is asleep – I start work. Work is always very busy.
3 o'clock – I have dinner at the hospital.

DAY

6 o'clock – The sun is coming up. I finish work and go home.
8 o'clock – My family has breakfast. I'm usually very tired, and I go to sleep.
4 o'clock – My children come home from school. I get up and have breakfast. Sometimes I clean up the house.
5 o'clock – I usually help my children with their homework, then I go for a walk.

6 Make sentences about Anna's routine. Use *always*, *sometimes*, or *never*.

> She always goes home at six o'clock.

> She never has breakfast at seven o'clock.

7 Project — Choose a job that people do at night. Write a diary for their day or night.

A Police Officer's Diary

Night
6 o'clock – I wake up and have breakfast.
7 o'clock – I feed the dog, and then I bike to work.
9 o'clock – I usually have a break and drink some tea.
12 o'clock – I have a sandwich for lunch.
5 o'clock – I finish work, and I sometimes have dinner with the other police officers.

Portfolio

Talk and Find Out

Helping at Home

1 Make a prediction.

I predict that there are _____ children in my class who sometimes _____.

2 Read and check ✓ *Yes* or *No*.

Yes / No

1. Do you sometimes cook? ☐ / ☐
2. Do you sometimes do the dishes? ☐ / ☐
3. Do you sometimes clean your room? ☐ / ☐
4. Do you sometimes dry the dishes? ☐ / ☐
5. Do you sometimes help with the shopping? ☐ / ☐
6. Do you sometimes wash your clothes? ☐ / ☐

3 Ask and answer. *Who sometimes cooks?*

4 Make a table and write a report.

	Yes	No		Yes	No
stove	12	9	apron	17	4
sink	15	6	shopping	14	7
clothes	18	3	laundry	7	14

> I predicted that there are 10 children who sometimes cook at home. Now I know that there are 12 children who sometimes cook at home, and there are 9 children who never cook at home.

Communication

3 Think and Write

My Family

1 Write a list of things people in your family do.

My Mom	My Sister	I
works on the computer	goes to school	go to ...

2 Underline each word in your list in a color to show how often people do it.

always   usually   sometimes

3 What do the people in your family do on the weekend?

My mom always works on the computer.
My sister never makes breakfast ...
I sometimes go to ...

4 Write a poem and add photos or drawings. Use the text to help you.

Writing Tip
Poems are nice if they rhyme.

I always go to school on Mondays,
I usually ... on Tuesdays,
I sometimes ... on Wednesdays,
I like doing things that way.
I always ... on Thursdays,
I usually ... on Fridays,
But I never ... on the weekend,
Because that's the time to play.

Writing 45

4 Around Town

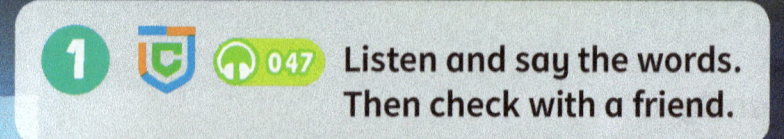

1 🎧 047 Listen and say the words. Then check with a friend.

1. bank
2. tower
3. fair
4. library
5. market
6. supermarket
7. bus station
8. parking lot
9. sports center
10. map

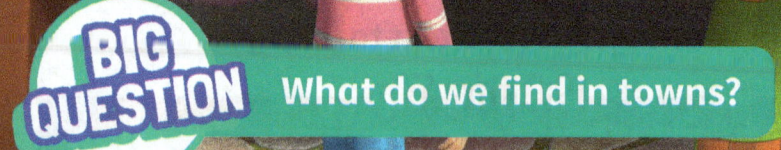

BIG QUESTION What do we find in towns?

Go up high in the town. See the letter when you look down.

2 🎧 048 Listen and answer.

1 Where do Ben and Lucy want to go?
2 Who do they ask?
3 Where is the tower?
4 What does the woman tell them to look at?

3 Look at the map. Ask and answer.

Where is the shoe store?

It's next to the parking lot, between the bus station and the sports center.

46 Towns

1 Look, read, and draw lines.

a

b

1 The school is across from the park.
2 The clock is above the window.
3 The map is close to the library.
4 The clock is below the window.

c

d

2 Where do the words go? Say the sentences.

1 The bus stop is the supermarket. (close to)
2 The parking lot is the library. (across from)
3 The clock is the map. (above)
4 The bus station is the tower. (below)

3 🎧 049 Watch, listen, and say.

Language Focus

The library is over there.
It's **across from** the park, **close to** the bank.
Below the sports center there's a door.
The library's **above** it, on the third floor.

4 Play the guessing game.

I'm thinking of a place. It's across from the bank. What is it?

I think it's the fair.

That's right!

Prepositions

1 🎧 050 ▶ **Listen and write the two places the singer cannot find. Then sing the song.**

1 _____   2 _____

Across from the library,
In the square,
I'm looking for the bank,
But it's not there.

Just below the tower,
Near the store,
My map says there's a café,
But there is not.

In front of the station,
In the street,
There's a place
Where people always meet.

I'm waiting here,
For Jennifer and Kate,
But they're already
Three hours late.

Excuse me, can you help me find my way?
I'm getting lost everywhere I go today.
I don't really understand this town.
Of course you don't!
Your map is upside down!

2 🛡 **Play the town game.**

> Close your eyes. Imagine you can see a town. There's a big library. What's close to it?

> Near the library, there's an old school. You close your eyes. Imagine the old school. What's across from it?

3 🛡 **Draw and write about your imaginary town.**

48 Singing for Pleasure

1 🎧 052 Listen and number.

a   b   c   d

2 Put the words in order. Say the sentences.
1 buy   the store   I'm   going to   to   some bread.
2 I'm   to   basketball.   the sports center   play   going to

3 ▶ 🎧 053 Watch, listen, and say.

Language Focus

I'm going to the library to get a book.
I'm going to the market to get some food.
I'm going to the station to go away.
On vacation, a cool vacation!

4 Where are you going? Complete the sentences. Then act it out.
1 I'm going to the supermarket ___to buy___ some apples.
2 I'm going to the sports center _____ swimming.
3 I'm going to my friend's house _____ TV.
4 I'm going to the library _____ a book.
5 I'm going to the supermarket _____ a drink.
6 I'm going to my grandma's _____ in the kitchen.

to read   ~~to buy~~
to go   to buy
to watch   to help

Where are you going?

I'm going to the … to …
What about you?

Be going to + Infinitive of Purpose **49**

Up High

1 🔊 054 ▶ **What is higher than the tower?**

1.
Zelda: They're going to the tower.
Lucy: Let's hurry, Ben. The tower's close to the market.
Ben: OK. Come on, Buster.

2.
Lucy: Look, the tower's over there, close to the school. The next letter's waiting for us!
Ben: Wow! There's a fair!

3.
Ben: Let's go to the fair.
Lucy: Sorry, Ben. We're going to the tower to get the next letter. No time to play!

4.
Ben: Come on, Lucy!
Lucy: Mmm. The tower is high ... but the Pirate Ship is higher.

5.
Ben: Lucy! Where are you going?
Lucy: I'm going to the fair to get the next letter!
Ben: What?

6.
Lucy: Let's go on the Pirate Ship. Quick!
Ben: The Pirate Ship?

Value: Lateral Thinking; Reading for Pleasure

7

Ben: We're above the tower!
Lucy: Yes, we're really high now. It's scary!
Ben: There's the letter. Look!
Lucy: It's an *R*. Great!

8

Horax: Oh, no!
Zelda: We're in the wrong place!

2 Read and find the pictures in the story. Then answer.

1 Find a picture where someone is excited. What makes them excited? _____
2 Find a picture where someone is scared. What are they scared of? _____
3 Find a picture where someone is angry. What makes them angry? _____
4 Find a picture where someone is happy. What makes them happy? _____

Phonics

3 Find who says …   *It's an R. Great!*

4 🎧 055 Listen and say.

Rory, **R**eery, and **R**ury – **r**obots in a f**ar** away superm**ar**ket.

Phonics Focus: /ar/ and /r/

Skills

1 Look and read the sentences. Write words.

market

map

bus stop

castle

bank

sports center

library

parking lot

1 People go there to get money. _____
2 It's old, and often next to a town. _____
3 This is a place where you go to find interesting books. _____
4 It's a good place to buy fruit and vegetables. _____
5 You go there to play soccer and basketball and to go swimming. _____
6 You need it in a town when you are new. It helps you find places. _____

1 🎧 056 Listen and find out where the robots are going. Write C (Caroline), M (Mark), E (Elly), and R (Robert).

2 Ask and answer.

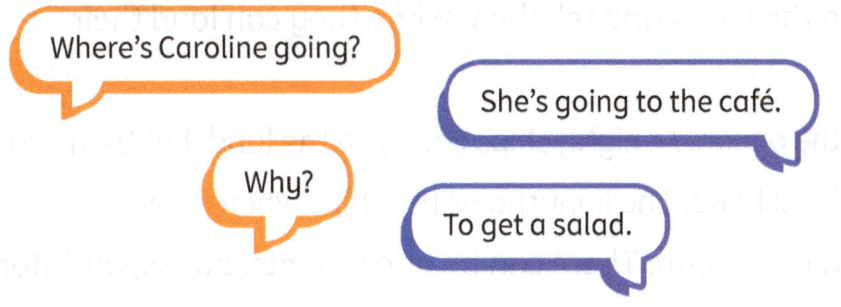

 Where's Caroline going?

 She's going to the café.

 Why?

 To get a salad.

3 Imagine a robot. Write where he/she is going and why.

 This is Roro. He is going to the parking lot to get his super sports car.

Listening, Speaking, and Writing

Think and Learn

TALL BUILDINGS

▶ Why are some buildings tall?

Super Fact!
The world's first skyscraper is in Chicago, U.S.A. They finished building it in 1885.

1 🎧 057 Listen and point.

1. lighthouse
2. skyscraper
3. airport tower
4. clock tower

2 Read and write the names of the buildings.

1. The people in this building can see planes flying, landing, and moving around the airport. They talk to the pilots and tell them when they can land their planes. _____

2. This building is close to the ocean. At night, ships can't see the land, but they can see the light at the top of this building. The light shows the ships where to go. _____

3. This big building is usually in a city. There can be apartments, banks, and stores in this building. _____

4. This building can be in a city or a town. The building tells people what time it is. _____

3 Look at the buildings in Activity 1 again. Why do you think they're tall? Choose a, b, or c.

It's tall …

a so that people can see the building from far away.
b so that people can see lots of things outside the building.
c so that there can be lots of things inside the building.

> The lighthouse is tall so that …

54 Geography

4 Why do you think these buildings are tall?

I think building 1 is tall so that …

1

2

3

5 What tall buildings are in your town? Why do you think they are tall?

There's a … in my town. It's tall so that …

6 Project Design a tall building. Describe it and say why it's tall. Tell your friends.

This is a skyscraper. It's very tall so that there can be lots of things inside it. There are apartments and stores. There's a swimming pool, too!

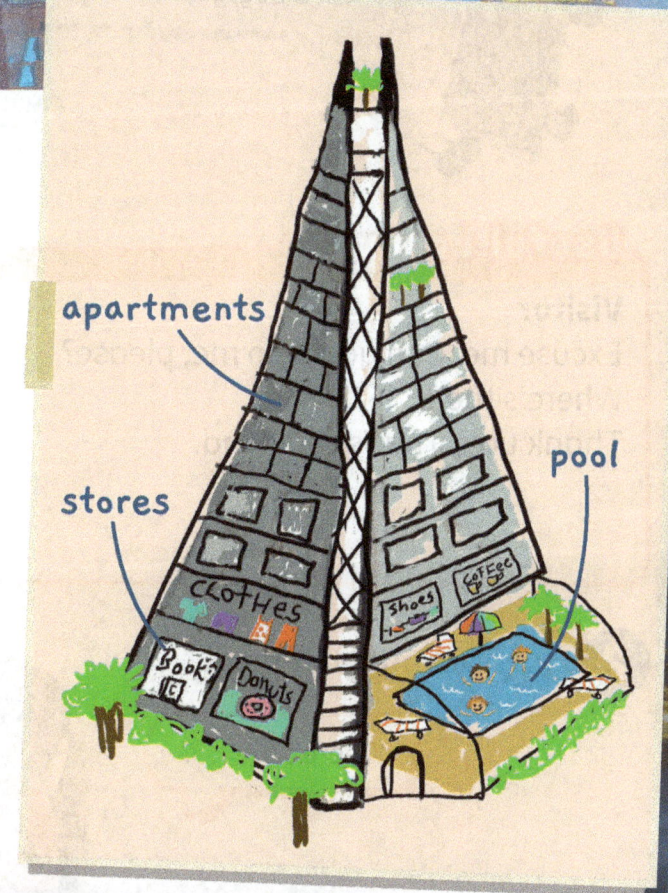

apartments

stores

pool

Geography

Portfolio

Talk and Find Out

Help a Visitor in Your Town

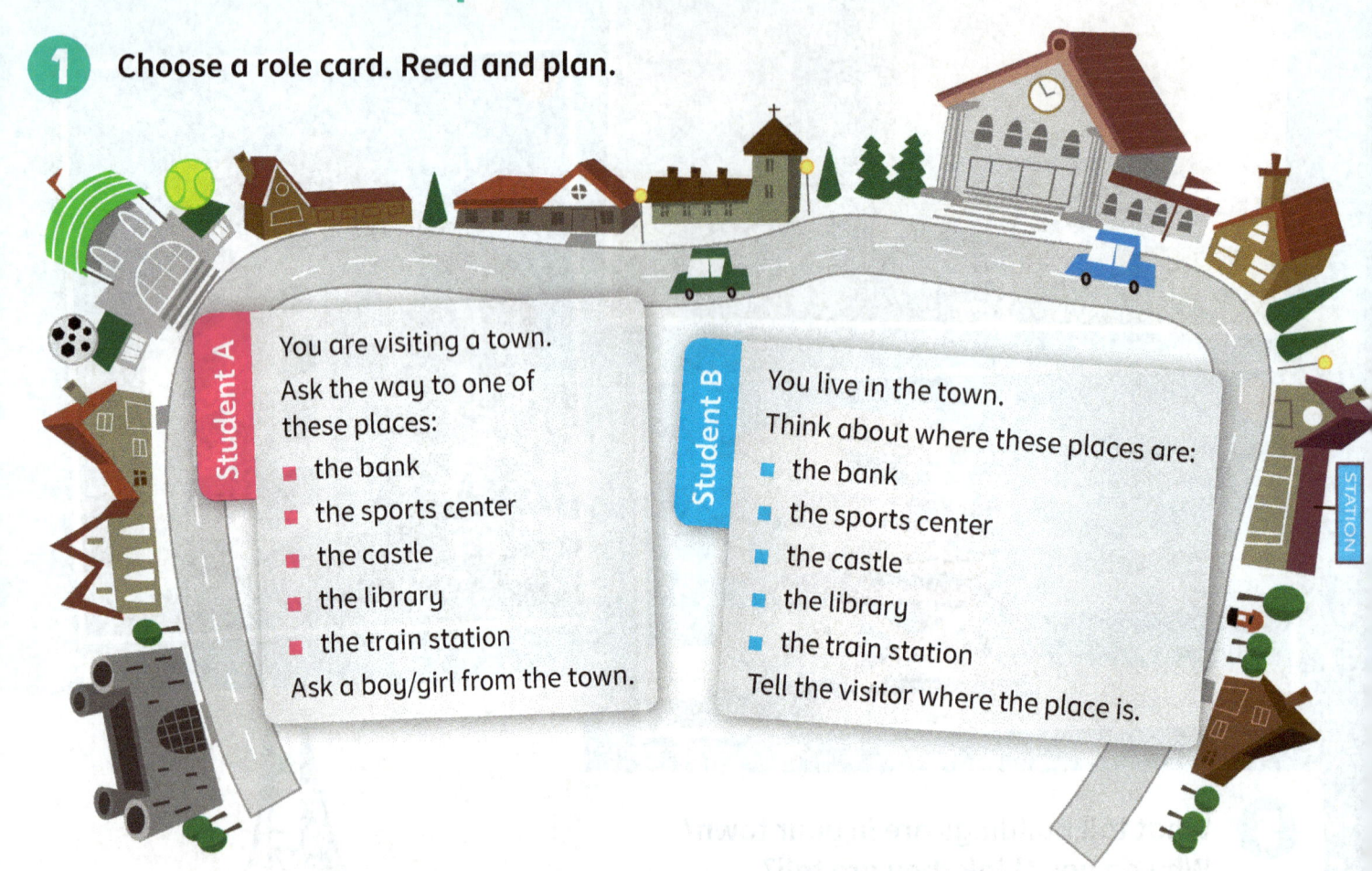

1 Choose a role card. Read and plan.

Student A
You are visiting a town.
Ask the way to one of these places:
- the bank
- the sports center
- the castle
- the library
- the train station

Ask a boy/girl from the town.

Student B
You live in the town.
Think about where these places are:
- the bank
- the sports center
- the castle
- the library
- the train station

Tell the visitor where the place is.

Useful Language

Visitor
Excuse me. Can you help me, please?
Where's the … ?
Thank you. That's very kind.

Boy/Girl
Yes, of course.
I'm sorry. I don't know.
No problem! The … is across from / next to / below / between the …
You're welcome!

2 Act out your play.

Where's the … ?

It's …

56 Communication

Think and Write

Messages

1. Use the code to find out what the messages mean.

A	B	C	D	E	F	G	H	I	J	K	L	M
☿	↗	⊙	☾	Ⅱ	♁	○	✱	⊼	?	◐	✶	♍

N	O	P	Q	R	S	T	U	V	W	X	Y	Z
☽	ᐯ	♄	♎	⟲	⊻	≈	Ω	⊿	●	♃	∝	♋

_ _ _ _   _ _ _   _ _ _   _ _ _ _ _ ?

WHAT ARE YOU DOING?

_ ' _   _ _ _ _ _   _ _   _ _ _   _ _ _ _ _ _ _

_ _   _ _ _ _   _   _ _ _ _ .

I'M GOING TO THE LIBRARY TO READ A BOOK.

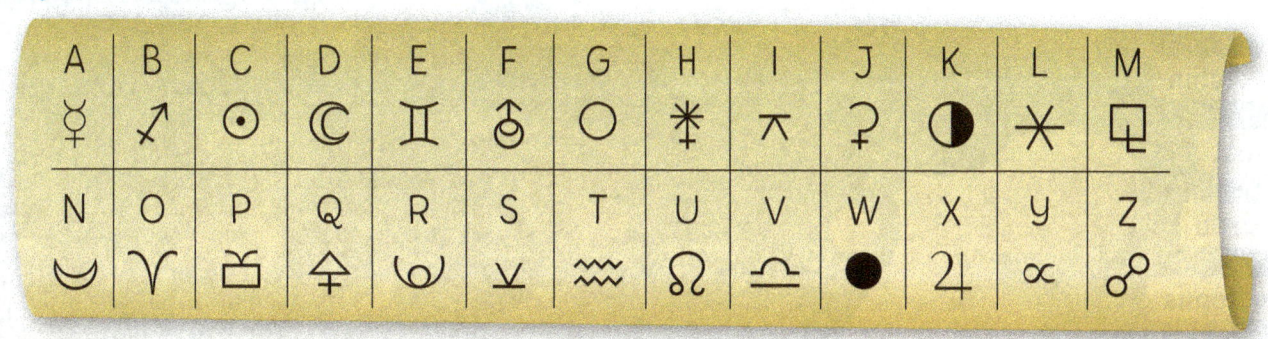

2. Imagine you are in a town. Write where you are at the different times.

> 9 o'clock: I'm in the library.
>
> 10 o'clock: I'm in the café.
>
> 11 o'clock: I'm in the shoe store.
>
> 12 o'clock: I'm in the bank.
>
> 2 o'clock: I'm going home.

3. People are writing you text messages. Write their messages and your answers.

> **What are you doing?** — Mom – 9:00
>
> **Hi Mom. I'm going to the library to get a book.** — Me – 9:05

Writing Tip
Remember that text messages can be very short!

5 Under the Ocean

1 🎧 058 Listen and say the words. Then check with a friend.

1. dolphin
2. seal
3. turtle
4. octopus
5. anchor
6. starfish
7. shell
8. seahorse

BIG QUESTION What's in the ocean?

By diving down and getting wet, another letter you will get.

2 🎧 059 Listen and correct the sentences.

1. Ben doesn't like the ocean.
2. Lucy thinks the letter is under the ocean.
3. The children think the octopus is ugly.
4. Lucy is worried about Horax and Zelda.

3 Play the chain game.

> There's a shark in the swimming pool.

> There's a shark and a seahorse in the swimming pool.

58 Ocean Creatures

1 🎧 060 Listen, read, and write the missing words.

The Golden Toad

Many years ago, in the forests of Costa Rica, there were many golden toads. There were beautiful pools in the forest. These pools were the (1) _____ for the babies of the golden toads. 1987 was very hot. Soon, there was no (2) _____ in the pools. Now there are no more golden toads.

The Megalodon

Megalodons were sharks. They were very, very (3) _____. They weren't very fast. Three million years ago, the oceans got colder. There wasn't any (4) _____ for the megalodons. Two million years ago, there were no more megalodons.

2 Where do the words go? Say the sentences.

1 The golden toad from Costa Rica. (was)
2 Before 1987, it so hot. (wasn't)
3 Megalodons very fast swimmers. (weren't)
4 They very big and very heavy. (were)

3 ▶ 🎧 061 Watch, listen, and say.

Language Focus

Greg **was** on a beach.
There **weren't** any people.

But then there **were** bees.
Then he **wasn't** happy.

4 Talk about the dinosaurs.

gray   big   brown   blue   small   orange

It was small …

Was / Were 59

1 🎧 062 ▶ Listen and check ✓ the ocean creatures that are in the song. Then sing the song.

☐   ☐   ☐   ☐   ☐   ☐

Deep under the dark, blue ocean,
In between the rocks,
There was an awful animal.
Its name was Crocorox.

**Swim, swim, swim, swim, swim away.
Swim away from here!
The crocorox is dangerous.
The crocorox is near!
Bad old Crocorox.**

Its face was square and ugly.
Its eyes were small and red.
Its teeth were long and horrible.
There were scales on its head.

Swim, swim, swim …

The starfish were all very scared.
The octopus was sad.
The turtle hid inside its shell.
That crocorox was bad.

Help!
Swim, swim, swim, swim, swim away.
Swim away right now!
The crocorox is hungry.
The crocorox is … Ow!

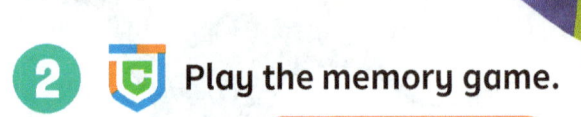

2 Play the memory game.

> Its eyes were blue.

> No, they weren't. They were red.

Singing for Pleasure

5

1 🎧 064 Look, listen, and draw lines. Who ate the cake?

Sally
Bob
Spike
Alice
Sue
Judy
Tim

2 Match the questions and answers.

1 Were you in the ocean, Julia?
2 Was Paul at the beach?
3 Where were you, Maria?
4 Were there shells on the beach?
5 Was there a shark in the ocean?

a I was in the ocean.
b No, there wasn't.
c Yes, there were.
d No, I wasn't.
e Yes, he was.

3 🎧 065 Watch, listen, and say.

Language Focus

Were you at the beach, Greg?
Yes, I **was**.
Were you in the ocean, Greg?
No, I **wasn't**.

Were there turtles?
No, there **weren't**.
Was there a shark?
No, there **wasn't**.

4 🛡 Play the guessing game.

Guess where I was yesterday at five?

Were you in the park?

Questions and Answers with *Was / Were* 61

The Trap

1 🎧 066 ▶ Which animal chases Horax?

1
Lucy: I can't see a letter.
Ben: What about that giant shell over there?
Lucy: Good idea. Maybe the letter's in there.
Ben: Let's take a look.

2
Lucy: Hurry up, Ben. Is there a letter there?
Ben: No, I don't think so.
Lucy: Let's look in a different place.

3
Ben: Help, Lucy! I can't get my arm out. I'm stuck.
Lucy: I'm sorry, Ben. I can't open the shell.

4
Ben: Oh, no! It's Horax and Zelda.
Lucy: And a shark! I'm scared.
Horax: Come out, my beauty.

5
Zelda: I don't think the shark is very happy with us, Horax.
Horax: What! Not me, you stupid shark. The children. Get the children!

6
Horax: Help! Help!
Ben: That shark doesn't like Horax.
Lucy: No. I don't think he was happy in Horax's cage.

62 Reading for Pleasure

7

Ben: Thank you, octopus. You're very helpful.
Lucy: Finally. Now we can go and find that letter.

8

Lucy: Look! Look at the fish.
Ben: It's the letter *S*!
Lucy: Now we have our fourth letter.

2 Read and draw lines to make sentences.

1 Lucy and Ben
2 Ben
3 Horax
4 The shark
5 The octopus
6 The fish

a has a shark in a cage.
b helps Ben escape.
c gets stuck in a big shell.
d make the letter S.
e are looking for the letter.
f doesn't like Horax and Zelda.

Phonics

3 Find who says … *I'm **s**orry, Ben. I can't open the **sh**ell.*

4 🎧 067 Listen and say.

Shane is **s**uper **s**cared. There's a **sh**ark in the **s**wimming pool.

Phonics Focus: *s* and *sh*

Skills / Storytime

1 Look at the pictures and the title. What do you think the story is about? Write three sentences. Share them with the class.

I think the story is about … There is / are …

2 🎧 068 Read and listen. Check your answers.

Saved by Dolphins

Kylie Morgan is on vacation with her mom and dad on the North Island of New Zealand.

One morning, her dad asks, "Who wants to go for a swim in the ocean?"

"I do!" says Kylie.

"I want to sit on the beach and read my book," says her mom.

Kylie and her dad are swimming in the ocean.

"Look!" shouts Kylie. "There's a dolphin."

Soon, there are four big dolphins in the water next to them. They are swimming in circles around Kylie and her dad.

"I think they want to play with us," says Kylie.

The circle of dolphins gets smaller and smaller. They are now very close to Kylie and her dad. Then, the dolphins start to hit their tails on the top of the water. Up and down, up and down.

"This is fun," laughs Kylie. But her dad is worried. "Why are the dolphins doing this?" he thinks. But he doesn't say anything to Kylie.

Then he sees something. Behind the dolphins, there is a big, gray fin swimming through the water. Kylie's dad knows what it is. It's the fin of a great white shark.

Value: Being Brave; Reading Skills

Great white sharks can be very big, and they have hundreds of teeth in their huge mouths. They can swim very fast, and they eat other ocean animals like fish, seals, turtles, and birds.

Kylie's dad knows all this. That is why he is scared. He pulls Kylie close to him, but he still doesn't say anything.

For ten minutes, Kylie's dad watches the fin swimming around them. Then it swims away. The dolphins stop swimming in circles, and Kylie and her dad can swim back to the beach.

On the beach, Kylie's dad tells Kylie and her mom about the shark.

"Those dolphins really helped us!" he says.

3 Complete the sentences.

1 Kylie _____Morgan_____ is with her parents on vacation.
2 Kylie's mom doesn't want to go for a _____.
3 Kylie sees some _____ in the ocean.
4 Kylie's dad doesn't tell her about the _____.
5 The shark stays near them for _____.
6 Kylie's dad thinks the dolphins _____ them.

4 069 Listen to a summary of the story. Write the four differences.

In the summary we have …

1 _____sleeps_____ instead of _____reads her book_____.
2 _____ instead of _____.
3 _____ instead of _____.
4 _____ instead of _____.

FACT FILE:
Great White Shark
- They can grow _____.
- They have _____.
- They can swim _____.
- They eat _____.

5 Talk together: are all ocean animals dangerous?

Writing, Listening, and Speaking Skills

Think and Learn

People and the Ocean

▶ How do people endanger the ocean?

1 🎧 070 Listen and point.

1 plastic pollution
2 oil pollution
3 coral reef dying
4 ice melting

2 Look at the pairs of photos. How do these pictures make you feel? Draw faces: 😊 😐 😣

3 Talk about the pictures. Use the words below to help you.

1 ocean / clean / no plastic
2 ocean / not clean / plastic
3 beach / clean
4 beach / dirty / lots of oil

5 coral reef / beautiful colors / fish
6 coral reef / white / no fish
7 ice / lots of
8 ice / smaller

> In the first picture, the ocean is clean, and there isn't any plastic.

> The ocean in the second picture isn't clean. There's … .

66 Environmental Studies

4 🎧 071 Listen, read, and write the words in the correct spaces.   Pollution   Climate Change

OUR SICK OCEANS

Our oceans are very important. Millions of ocean creatures live in them. Ocean plants make 50% of our oxygen and take 25% of our carbon dioxide. But our oceans are in danger.

A _____

The world is getting hotter, and the ice at the north and south poles is melting (becoming water). Because there is more water in the ocean, there are more floods, and many cities by the ocean are in danger.

The ocean is also getting hotter. This is bad for coral reefs because the hotter water is killing the coral. The coral is losing its beautiful colors and turning white. Ocean creatures can't live in it any more, and lots of starfish, seahorses, and other fish are losing their homes.

B _____

Plastic pollution is a big problem for our oceans. There is lots of plastic trash, like bags and cups, in the water. Ocean creatures sometimes eat the plastic. Lots of fish now have plastic inside them.

There are lots of big boats and ships on our oceans. They take things like clothes, televisions, food, and people around the world. There is pollution from their oil in the water. Fish and coral reefs are dying from this pollution. Ships can also hit coral reefs.

5 ⭐ Project What can you do to stop climate change and ocean pollution? Make a leaflet.

I can stop using plastic bags.

How can we stop CLIMATE CHANGE and POLLUTION in the ocean?

Cafés can stop using plastic cups.

Environmental Studies

Portfolio

Talk and Find Out

Where Were We ... ?

1 Make a prediction.

_____ classmates were at home on Saturday afternoon.

2 Draw a table. Write in the names of the children from your group. Ask questions and write the answers in the table.

Name	Where Were You on Saturday Afternoon?
James	at the theater
Aruna	at home
Vee	in the swimming pool
Alice	at a friend's house

3 Write a list of all the places. Check ✓ the number of children and count them.

Place	Number of Children	Total
at the theater	✓	1
at home	✓✓✓✓✓	5
at the movies	✓✓	2
in a store	✓✓✓	3
at a friend's house	✓✓✓✓	4
at a party	✓	1
in the yard	✓✓✓✓	4
in the swimming pool	✓✓	2

4 Talk about your results.

- Was your prediction correct?
- No, it wasn't. Five classmates were at home on Saturday afternoon.

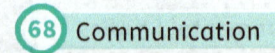

Communication

Think and Write

Ocean Creatures

1 Find information about an ocean creature and make notes.

Writing Tip
Making notes helps you write.

Animal: Turtle

- What do they look like? brown, green, yellow, gray, four legs, hard shell
- Where do they live? in water (salt water and fresh water)
- How do they have their young? lay eggs in the sand on the beach, then go away, babies open egg, start to swim
- How long do they live? 40-70 years, but the oldest turtle is about 175 years old!
- Other interesting facts: turtles have very good eyes, and they don't have ears.

2 Find pictures and write about your ocean creature.

TURTLES

I like turtles. They are beautiful. They are green, yellow, gray, and brown. They live in the ocean, rivers, or lakes. They eat plants and small animals. Turtles lay eggs on beaches. They put their eggs into the sand. The baby turtles swim. Turtles usually live for 40-70 years, but they can live up to 175 years.

6 Gadgets

1 🎧 072 Listen and say the words. Then check with a friend.

1. cell phone
2. tablet
3. electric toothbrush
4. elevator
5. flashlight
6. electric fan
7. walkie-talkie
8. laptop
9. game console

BIG QUESTION How are gadgets useful?

The next letter is underground. Go to the caves and look around.

2 🎧 073 Listen and answer.

1. Where is the next letter?
2. What is $12?
3. What do they buy?
4. Who do they see?

3 You are going on vacation. Decide what you want to buy.

Let's buy an electric toothbrush.

Oh yes, and how about an electric fan?

70 Technology

1
🎧 074 Listen and complete the table.

$80 $99   big   small

	Price ($)	Size
S2 20		
S5 30		

2
Complete with *beautiful*, *cheaper*, or *bigger*. Say the sentences.

1 The S5 30 is _____ than the S2 20.
2 The S2 20 is _____ than the S5 30.
3 The S5 30 is more _____ than the S2 20.

3
▶ 🎧 075 Watch, listen, and say.

Language Focus

My phone's **smaller than** yours.
Your phone's **more beautiful than** mine.
My phone's **bigger than** yours.
It's **more expensive than** yours.

4
Think of something in the classroom. Play the guessing game.

Is it more expensive than the scissors?

Is it smaller than the scissors?

Is it the clock?

Yes, it is.

No, it isn't.

Yes, it is.

Comparatives 71

1 🎧 076 ▶ Listen and match the buttons to the gadgets. Then sing the song.

Look at my gadget.
It's really cool.
It's bigger than yours,
More beautiful, too.

Press the red button.
The flashlight comes on.
Press the blue button.
It plays a song.

Look at my gadget.
It's really cool.
It's newer than yours,
More expensive, too.

Press the brown button.
The fan comes on.
Press the green button.
And call someone.

Look at my gadget.
It's really cool.
It's bigger than yours,
More beautiful, too.

2 Decide what happens when you press these buttons.

1. 2. 3.

3 Tell your friend about the buttons.

What happens when you press the purple button?

The walkie-talkie comes on. I use it to talk to my brother.

Singing for Pleasure

1 Read and number the pictures.

1 This is the fastest boat in the world. It can go at 511 km/h.

2 This is the most expensive watch in the world. It costs $58 million!

3 This is the tallest building in the world. It is 830m tall.

4 Is this the ugliest cat in the world? What do you think?

2 Put the words in order. Say the sentences.

1 is   the world.   This   the fastest   in   car

2 the most   house   expensive   the world.   in   is   This

3 🔊 078 Watch, listen, and say.

Language Focus

Our house is **the biggest** in the tree.
There's lots of room for Gina and me.
Our tree is **the tallest** in the woods.
Look at our tree. Life is good!
Our view is **the most beautiful** I know.
Careful, Greg. Watch where you go!

4 Complete the sentences. Tell your friend.

1 _____ is the tallest person in my family.

2 _____ is the most difficult subject in school.

3 _____ is the funniest person I know.

4 _____ is the most exciting show on TV.

5 _____ is the most beautiful place I know.

My aunt is the tallest person in my family.

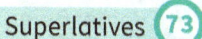

Superlatives

The Cave

1 🎧 079 ▶ What do Horax and Zelda hear in the cave?

1
Lucy: The book says go to the caves. Here we are.
Ben: Somewhere down there is the next letter.

2
Ben: Stay here and watch for Horax and Zelda.
Lucy: OK. Do you have your walkie-talkie and flashlight?
Ben: Yes. I have everything.

3
Ben: It's much darker down here. The flashlight was a good idea.
Lucy: Can you see the letter?
Ben: No, I can't.

4
Ben: Wow! What beautiful cave paintings! What's that? It's the letter *E*. *E* is the fifth letter in our puzzle.

5
Ben: Oh, no. It's Zelda and Horax. I have to hide!

6
Horax: Where are those kids?
Ben: Lucy, I have a problem. Horax and Zelda are here.
Lucy: Don't worry. I have an idea.

Value: Being Resourceful; Reading for Pleasure

7

Buster: Grrrrrr!
Zelda: What's that?
Horax: I don't know. I'm scared.
Zelda: Let's run!

8

Ben: Great idea, Lucy!
Lucy: Good job, Buster. You're the smartest dog in the world.

2 Write a quiz for the story. Here are the answers.

1 Go to the caves. _____?
2 Ben. _____?
3 Lucy. _____?
4 The letter *E*. _____?
5 Behind a rock. _____?
6 Buster. _____?

Phonics

3 Find who says ...   *What beautiful cave paintings!*

4 🎧 080 Listen and say.

Irene uses her phone to find the limes for her cake.

Phonics Focus: Long Vowel Sounds

Skills

1 **Read and circle.**

1 **Salesclerk:** Can I help you?
  Dan:
  a No, I can't help you.
  b Yes, I'd like to buy a flashlight.
  c Yes, I have a flashlight.

2 **Dan:** How much is this flashlight?
  Salesclerk:
  a It's $20.
  b It's 20 kg.
  c It's 20 cm.

3 **Dan:** Do you have a cheaper one?
  Salesclerk:
  a Yes, this one is $12.
  b It's cheaper than the walkie-talkie.
  c It's the most expensive.

4 **Dan:** I'd like to buy it.
  Salesclerk:
  a Come back tomorrow.
  b I have an idea.
  c Yes, of course.

5 **Dan:** Goodbye!
  Salesclerk:
  a Goodbye and thank you!
  b Yes, please.
  c Oh, no!

2 **Look at the pictures and talk about the differences.**

The fan in A is cheaper than the fan in B.

Reading and Speaking

1 🛡 **Look carefully. Close your books and say.**

> There are some sunglasses.

2 🎧 081 **Listen and check ✓ the gadgets that Ana has.**

3 🎧 082 **Listen again and complete the sentences.**

1 The sunglasses are also a _____.
2 The fan is also a _____.
3 The watch is also a _____.
4 Ana uses the electric toothbrush to _____ her _____.

4 🛡 **Choose a spy gadget. Draw a picture and write sentences about it.**

This is a spy tablet.
It is also a skateboard.
You can use it to escape!

Listening, Speaking, and Writing.

Think and Learn

CAVE PAINTINGS

▶ What materials did cave artists use in the past?

Super Fact!
The oldest cave painting in the world is in Indonesia. It's more than 40,000 years old. The painting is of a kind of cow.

1 🎧 083 Listen and point.

1. charcoal
2. rock powder
3. twig
4. lamp
5. cave ceiling

2 Read and answer the questions.

Long ago, cave artists liked painting pictures on the walls and ceilings of their caves. They used small lamps to see their paintings because it was very dark inside the caves. We can see very old paintings of animals and birds in some caves today, and sometimes the paintings tell a story.
The colors in cave paintings are usually black, red, yellow, orange, and brown. The color black comes from charcoal. Artists used this to draw the lines of the animals. The colors red, yellow, orange, and brown come from rock powder. Artists mixed the powder with water to make paint, and they used their fingers and small twigs from trees to put the paint on the cave walls.

1 Where were the cave paintings?
2 What was it like in the caves?
3 What did they paint?
4 Do the paintings tell a story?
5 What colors are in the cave paintings?
6 What did they use to put the paint on the walls?

3 What would you paint on a cave wall today?

Places: _my house_
Animals: _____
People: _____
Gadgets: _____

History

4 Look, read, and match.

Today, artists use pencils, brushes, and paints, but there weren't any of these things for cave artists.

Things Artists Use Today

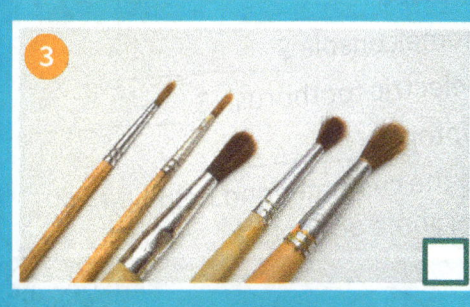

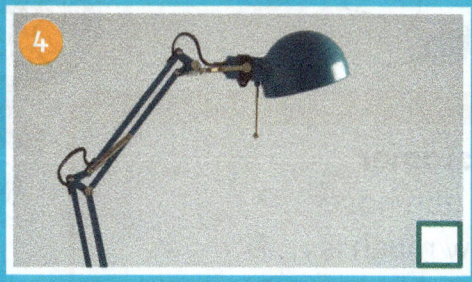

1.
2.
3.
4.

Things Cave Artists Used

a.
b.
c.
d.

5 🎧 084 Listen and check.

6 ⭐ Project Make a cave painting from life today. Write about your picture.

This is a cave painting of my house. That's me in my bedroom window.

History 79

Portfolio

Talk and Find Out

Go Shopping

1 Choose a role card. Read and plan.

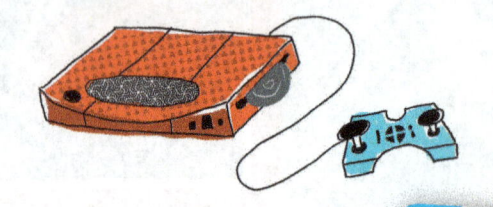

Student A
You are in a store. Choose three things you want to buy:
- a flashlight
- a walkie-talkie
- a tablet
- a game console
- an electric toothbrush
- a laptop

You have $100 to spend. Talk to the salesclerk and see what you can buy.

Student B
You are a salesclerk. Find out the prices from your teacher and write them:
- a flashlight $_____
- a walkie-talkie $_____
- a tablet $_____
- a game console $_____
- an electric toothbrush $_____
- a laptop $_____

Talk to the customer and help him/her buy some gadgets.

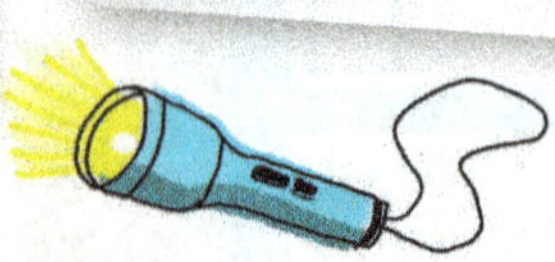

Useful Language

Salesclerk
Good morning/afternoon.
Can I help you?
Yes, we do. / No, we don't.
It's ... dollar(s).
Of course!

Customer
Do you have ... ?
How much is ... ?
All right, so can I buy it?
Thank you.

2 Act out your play.

Good morning. Can I help you?

Yes, do you have any flashlights?

Yes, we do.

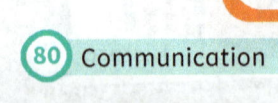

80 Communication

Think and Write

My Gadgets

1 Think of some toys or gadgets you have. Write words about them in a table.

Gadget	Got It When? Who From?	Looks?	Other Facts?
bike	birthday present, from my parents	red and black, bigger than old bike, very beautiful	bike to lots of places, sometimes to visit grandmother
cell phone	got with money from grandfather	small, silver, looks cool	listen to music before going to bed, love it!
camera	...	...	...

2 Tell your friend about your favorite gadget.

> It's my bike.
> I got it for my last birthday.
> I got it from my parents.

3 Write about your favorite gadget.

My favorite gadget is my bike.

It was my birthday present from my parents. My old bike was very small. This bike is bigger.

It's red and black. It's the most beautiful bike in the world.

I love my bike. I bike to lots of places on it. I sometimes ride my bike to visit my grandmother on the weekend.

Writing Tip

Read your writing slowly to check your spelling.

7 In the Hospital

1 🎧 085 Listen and say the words. Then check with a friend.

1. earache
2. headache
3. cold
4. toothache
5. stomachache
6. cough
7. doctor
8. nurse

BIG QUESTION What keeps us healthy?

Ben, your grandpa is sick. Go to the hospital now. Room 209. Come quickly!

2 🎧 086 Listen and correct the sentences.

1. The message says Lucy's dad is in the hospital.
2. Grandpa's room is downstairs.
3. The nurse shows them where the room is.
4. Ben and Lucy walk up the stairs.

3 Play the mime game.

What's the matter with me?   You have a stomachache.   That's right.

Health

1 🎧 087 Listen and number the pictures.

a b c d e

2 Look at Activity 1 again and write the correct words. Say the sentences.

play → played   shout → shouted   land → landed   jump → jumped

1 Yesterday, Harry _____ basketball.
2 He _____ up high.
3 He _____ on the floor.
4 "Ouch!" he _____.

3 ▶ 🎧 088 Watch, listen, and say.

Language Focus

Greg was in the yard and **looked** up at the tree.
Greg **shouted**, "Gina, come and climb with me!"
Gina **smiled** and said, "OK. That looks like fun!"
They **climbed**, then they **rested** in the hot, hot sun.
They **jumped** down from the tree, down into the pool.
They **landed** in the water – it was nice and cool.

4 Change the words to talk about yesterday. Ask and answer.

watch _ed_   listen ____   to visit ____   call ____   play ____   walk ____

What happened yesterday?

I watched a movie and played tennis. And you?

Simple Past: Regular Verbs 83

1 🎧 089 ▶ Listen and match. Then sing the song.

The doctor always tells me,
"An apple's good for you."
Well listen to my story.
It isn't always true.

I was in the kitchen.
There was an apple cake.
I swallowed it, but it was big.
I got a stomachache.

**It's not true! It's not true!
It isn't always true!
What the doctor tells me
isn't always true!**

I was at the apple farm.
I looked up at a snake!
I walked into an apple tree.
My head now really aches.

It's not true! It's not true! ...

I was at the market
With my family.
I took a box of apples, but
they landed on my knee.

It's not true! It's not true! ...

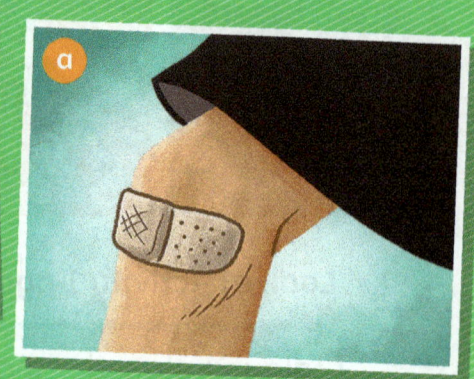

2 Look at the pictures above. Say what happened to the girl.

> First she ate a big apple cake. Then she …

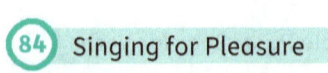

The next day, she …

There was / were …

She looked and …

…

3 Work with a partner. Close your eyes. Imagine what happened to the girl the next day.

84 Singing for Pleasure

7

1 Look, read, and complete the story.

Yesterday, I woke up early. I felt terrible. I had a bad **(1)**_____. I went to see the **(2)**_____ with my dad. She gave me some **(3)**_____. "No **(4)**_____ today," she said. "Great," I said. "No problem," said my dad. "Today is Saturday."

2 Look at Activity 1 again. Write the past form of the verbs.

1 wake up ➡ _____ up   3 have ➡ _____   5 give ➡ _____
2 feel ➡ _____   4 go ➡ _____   6 say ➡ _____

3 ▶ 🎧 091 Watch, listen, and say.

Language Focus

Greg **woke up** around half past eight.
He **felt** bad. He **had** a stomachache.
"You **had** too many flies," Mom **said**.
She **gave** him a drink, and he **went** back to bed.

4 Use the pictures to write a story about Millie.

Simple Past: Irregular Verbs 85

At the Hospital

1 🎧 092 ▶ Who saves Ben and Lucy?

1
Doctor: Here we are. Room 209. Go right in, kids. I'll see you and your grandfather later.
Ben: Thanks so much, Doctor.

2
Lucy: There's no answer. Your grandpa is sleeping.
Ben: OK, let's go in quietly.

3
Ben: Grandpa? Are you alright? I got a text message. It said you're in the hospital.
Lucy: Something isn't right.

4
Ben: Oh, no. It's a trap!
Lucy: Someone played a trick on us!

5
Horax: Ha, ha! It's so nice of you to visit me in the hospital. Welcome, children!
Ben: What do you want from us, Horax? Leave us alone!

6
Horax: You know what I want. I want the book, and I want the letters.
Lucy: No way! The book is ours. We found it in the castle!

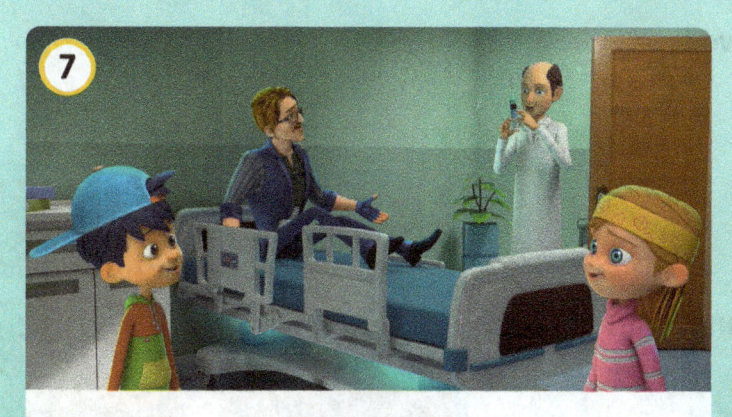

7
Doctor: Please go outside for a minute, kids. Your grandfather needs an injection.
Horax: Well, I'm … I mean … I'm not …
Doctor: Just lie down on the bed, please.

8
Lucy: Thanks, Doctor. We have to go now!
Ben: Bye-bye, Grandpa. Hope you get better soon!
Horax: Don't go! Wait! I want to …

2 Read and draw lines to make sentences.

1 Ben got
2 It said, "Go to the hospital,"
3 They found Horax
4 Horax wanted
5 At that moment,
6 Lucy and Ben said, "Bye-bye,"

a and not Ben's grandfather there!
b the book and the letters.
c the doctor came in.
d a text message.
e and went out of the room.
f but it was a trick.

Phonics

3 Find who says …

Someone play**ed** a trick on us!

4 🎧 093 Listen and say.

Mike hik**ed** – he lik**ed** it.

Kate skat**ed** – she hat**ed** it.

Phonics Focus: –ed Endings

Skills / Storytime

1 Read the story quickly. Write the answers.
  1. What is the girl's name?
  2. What was the girl's problem?
  3. What's the dog's name?

2 🎧 094 Read and listen. Check your answers.

A New Best Friend

Emma Woodward was 11 years old. She liked swimming and riding her bike. But one day Emma woke up with a headache. It got worse and worse, and Emma felt very sick. Her parents took her to a hospital, and she saw the doctor right away. Emma couldn't walk or stand up. The doctor looked at her very carefully. "There's a problem with Emma's head, she needs an operation right away."

After the operation, Emma was asleep. When she woke up, she had to stay in bed for a long time. She couldn't remember how to do anything. The doctor said, "Emma's legs are not strong. She needs to use a wheelchair. When she's not in the wheelchair, she needs crutches." Emma was very tired and didn't try to walk. "I can't do it!" she said. Her parents were worried. "What can we do? How can we help Emma?" they asked.

One day, Emma's mom heard about the Helper Dog Project. The project had dogs to help people with many different kinds of problems.

The next day, they went to see the Helper Dog Project. Emma was on her crutches. She went from the car to the building. She was very tired. She sat in a chair. Then one of the dogs came over. His name was Jasper, and he was the biggest dog in the room. He looked at Emma. Then he put his paw on Emma's leg. Emma knew Jasper was her new best friend.

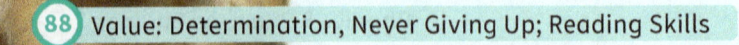

88 Value: Determination, Never Giving Up; Reading Skills

The family took Jasper home, and with his help Emma slowly learned to walk again. She put one hand on Jasper and used her other hand to hold a crutch. It was difficult, but every day, Emma walked a little more. Soon she started to walk with no crutches using Jasper to help her.

These days, Emma and Jasper are always together. Jasper even goes to school with Emma. When she is reading or writing, Jasper sleeps under her desk.

Last week, there was a surprise for Jasper and Emma. A magazine gave Jasper a big prize – The Best Animal of the Year! The next day, the story about the little girl and the big dog was in all the newspapers.

"Look!" Emma said to Jasper. "You are now the most famous dog in the world!"

Jasper looked at Emma. Then he put his paw on her leg. She remembered the first time she saw Jasper and smiled.

3 Put the story in order.

- [ ] Emma's mom and dad went to the Helper Dog Project with Emma.
- [ ] Emma liked the biggest dog, Jasper, a lot.
- [ ] Emma Woodward had a bad headache.
- [ ] Her parents took her to the hospital.
- [ ] Jasper got a big prize, The Best Animal of the Year!
- [ ] The doctor said, "You have to sit in a wheelchair or use crutches."
- [ ] With Jasper's help, Emma learned to walk again.

4 🎧 095 Listen to a summary of the story. Write the four differences.

In the summary we have …

1. ___stomachache___ instead of ___a headache___.
2. _____ instead of _____.
3. _____ instead of _____.
4. _____ instead of _____.

Think and Learn

STAYING HEALTHY

Super Fact! It's OK to eat unhealthy food sometimes. Just don't *always* eat it.

▶ How can we stay healthy?

1 🎧 096 Listen and point.

1. exercise
2. healthy food
3. unhealthy food
4. sleep
5. rest
6. fresh air

2 Read about healthy food, exercise, fresh air, and rest. Then write.

Eating healthy food, exercising, and getting fresh air and rest help us stay healthy.

Healthy Food
Try to eat some fruit and vegetables and some bread, pasta, or rice every day. Don't eat a lot of the same food, like chips, pizza, or ice cream.

Rest
Rest is also very important. You can rest by doing things like reading a book. The best way to rest is to sleep. That's why it's important to get good sleep every night.

Fresh Air
Go outside and get some fresh air! You can bike to school or to a friend's house.

Exercise
Try to exercise often to stay strong. Swimming, biking, and playing sports make us healthy. You can exercise with friends.

1. Write four examples of healthy food.
2. Write four ways of getting exercise.
3. Write two outdoor activities.
4. Write two ways of getting rest.

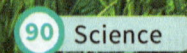

Science

3 Put these activities into the correct column.

swimming   playing computer games for four hours   always going to bed very late
always eating ice cream for lunch   walking to school   laughing with friends

HEALTHY	UNHEALTHY

4 Look at the pictures. Write *healthy* or *unhealthy*.

a _____   b _____   c _____   d _____

5 Match the sentences with the pictures in Activity 4.

1 These are bad for the teeth. ☐
2 It gets me outdoors. ☐
3 Sometimes it makes my eyes ache. ☐
4 I always make healthy food. ☐

6 Tell your partner about two things you do to stay healthy.

I play soccer to stay healthy.

I play tennis to stay healthy. I usually play tennis with my friends on Saturdays.

7 **Project** Make a storyboard or slide presentation to show how you stay healthy. Write some words in each box or on each slide.

Science

Portfolio

Talk and Find Out

At the Doctor's

1 Choose a role card. Read and plan.

Student A
You are the doctor. A patient is coming to see you.
- Ask what the problem is.
- Ask what happened.
- Check the problem.
- Say what the patient has to do.

Student B
You are the patient.
- You have a pain. Decide what the problem is.
- Tell the doctor what happened.
- Tell the doctor where you have the pain.
- Tell the doctor what you want to do tomorrow.

Useful Language

Doctor
What's the matter?
What happened?
Let me see.
You have to take some medicine / drink lots of water / stay in bed …
No problem. / No, you can't. You have to …

Patient
I have a pain in my …
I kicked … / jumped … / landed on …
Ouch!
Yes, of course. I want to play … / go … tomorrow. Is that OK?

2 Act out your play.

"Good morning, Doctor."

"Good morning. What's the matter?"

Communication

Think and Write

Write a Story

1 Think of a story. It can be a true story or a story you imagine. Use the questions to help you.

Writing Tip

Write stories in the past tense. Remember to check your verbs!

Who is the story about?	Tom, 12 years old, good swimmer
When?	3 weeks ago, Sunday
What was the weather like?	very sunny, hot
What happened?	swimming, jumped into pool, problem, not a lot of water, hurt his head, hospital, 3 weeks

2 Plan and write notes about your story. Draw pictures.

Tom – great swimmer.	Sunday, three weeks ago – sunny and very hot.	Tom jumped into the pool.
Not a lot of water.	Tom hurt his head.	Tom was in the hospital for 3 weeks.

3 Draw and write a story.

Tom loved swimming. He was very good at it.

One Sunday, it was very hot, and Tom wanted to swim. He jumped into the pool, but there was not much water in it.

8 Around the World

1 🎧 097 Listen and say the words. Then check with a friend.

1. Egypt
2. Argentina
3. India
4. Australia
5. Mexico
6. Brazil
7. Chile
8. Spain
9. China
10. Turkey

Come and see the model village. Travel the world in a day!

BIG QUESTION What wonders of the world are there?

Stay at home but travel far. The missing letter is where you are.

2 🎧 098 Listen and answer.

1. Who had the idea to go to the park?
2. How much is one ticket?
3. How much change does Lucy get?
4. Where does Ben want to go first and why?

3 Play the flag game.

- It's yellow and green.
- Egypt.
- Wrong. One point for me.

94 Countries

1 🎧 099 Listen and check ✓ the pictures.

1 Sara went …   **2** She saw …   **3** She ate …

a   a   a

b   b   b

2 Where do the words go? Say the sentences.

1 I went to the zoo with my mom, but dad go with us. (didn't)
2 We went to a pizza restaurant, but I have a pizza. (didn't)

3 ▶ 🎧 100 Watch, listen, and say.

Language Focus

I went to the ocean, but I **didn't have** fun.
The beach was cold, so I **didn't stay** for long.

4 Play the chain game.

We went on vacation, but we didn't eat ice cream.

We went on vacation, but we didn't eat ice cream, and we didn't go into the ocean.

Negatives with Simple Past

1 🎧 101 ▶ Listen and match the countries with the pictures. Then sing the song.

All the wonders in the world,
I didn't see a single one.
All the wonders in the world,
I was having too much fun.

I went to China,
But I didn't see the wall.
In India,
I didn't see the Taj Mahal.

All the wonders in the world …

I went to Egypt,
But I didn't see the Sphinx.
I went to Spain,
But I didn't see a lynx.

All the wonders in the world …

I went to Australia,
But I didn't see the sun.
And in Brazil,
I didn't see the Amazon.

All the wonders in the world …

1.  China
2. India
3. Egypt
4. Spain
5. Brazil

a. The Sphinx
b. The Amazon
c. A lynx
d. The Great Wall
e. The Taj Mahal

2 Make a list of wonders in your country.

I think the national museum is a wonder.

3 Compare with a friend.

I think the panda is a wonder.

96 Singing for Pleasure

1 🎧 103 Match the questions with the answers. Then listen and check.

1 Did you have fun in New York?
2 Who did you go with?
3 How long did you stay there?
4 Where did you stay?
5 Did you go to the Guggenheim Museum?
6 Did you send me a postcard?

☐ No, I didn't. We didn't have time.
☐ For a week.
☐ Yes, I did. It was great.
☐ Sorry! I forgot.
☐ Mom and Dad and Bobby.
☐ In a hotel close to Central Park.

2 Put the words in order. Say the sentences.

1 have you Did vacation? a good
2 did there? you Who see
3 How get there? you did
4 get you When home? did back

3 ▶ 🎧 104 Watch, listen, and say.

Language Focus

Did you **go** to Spain, Greg?
Yes, I **did**.
Did you **go** by plane, Greg?
No, I **didn't**.

When **did** you **get** home, Greg?
Yesterday.

4 Ask your friend questions about their last vacation.

Where … ?
… have fun?
How long … ?
How did you … ?
Who … go with?

Questions and Answers with Simple Past

The Final Letters

1 🎧 105 ▶ What are Ben and Lucy doing when Horax takes the book?

1
Lucy: What a great soccer stadium!
Ben: Yes, I'd love to go to Rio de Janeiro!
Lucy: Where next?
Ben: You choose.

2
Ben: The Great Wall of China. It's amazing!
Lucy: Yes, it is. But where are these letters? Do you have any idea, Ben?
Ben: Not yet, but let's keep looking.

3
Ben: What's this?
Lucy: It's the Opera House in Sydney, in Australia.

4
Ben: Hey, look. It's Mr. Williams.
Mr. Williams: Hi, kids. What are you doing here?
Lucy: Hello! We're learning about the world.
Mr. Williams: Well, have a good day.

5
Lucy: The Pyramids and the Sphinx. Cool!
Ben: But still no letters. Where can they be?

6
Ben: I'm hungry. I didn't have a very big breakfast this morning.
Lucy: I'm glad we made these sandwiches.

Value: Showing Interest in Other Cultures; Reading for Pleasure

Lucy: The book! It isn't here!
Ben: What happened? Did you drop it?
Lucy: I'm not sure. What can we do?

Ben: We have to go and look for the book.
Lucy: Maybe not! I can see the missing letters!
Ben: What? The *I*, *I*, and *A*?
Lucy: No, the *N* and *D*!

2 Look, read, and answer.

In which picture do they visit … ?

Phonics

3 Find who says … It's the Opera House in S**y**dn**ey**, in Australia.

4 🎧 106 Listen and say.

Sill**y** Mill**y** made a p**y**ramid of jam at the g**y**m.

Phonics Focus: /i/ and /ɪ/

Skills

1 🎧 **107** Listen and draw lines.

Daisy   Mary   Vicky   Fred

Peter   Paul   Jack

2 Read and write the words.

The Great Pyramid of Khufu **(1)** _____ in Giza, near Cairo. The ancient Egyptians built **(2)** _____ 5,000 years ago. It is about 140 meters high. It was the **(3)** _____ building in the world for a very long time. In **(4)** _____ of the pyramid is the Sphinx. It has the body of a lion and the head **(5)** _____ a man.

1	**a** are	**b** is	**c** am
2	**a** it	**b** them	**c** him
3	**a** tall	**b** taller	**c** tallest
4	**a** behind	**b** next	**c** front
5	**a** by	**b** on	**c** of

1 Read and talk about the questions.

You win a competition. The prize is a trip around the world.

You have one year, and you can visit six countries.

You can take one person with you.
- Which countries do you want to visit?
- How do you want to travel?
- What do you want to see?
- Who do you want to take with you?

2 Read Megan's travel blog. Match each day with a photo.

Megan's Travel Blog

a Day _____

b Day _____

c Day _____

Day 34
Today, we saw an amazing waterfall. It's called the Iguazu Falls. There was so much water! And it was really loud. We also visited three countries in one day. The Iguazu Falls are in Brazil and Argentina (and close to Paraguay, too!)

Day 78
Paris is the most beautiful city in the world, and today I saw the Eiffel tower. I took loads of photos. We didn't go up because we were very tired, but we're going to tomorrow. We already have our tickets.

Day 187
This is our second day on safari. The animals are amazing. Yesterday, we saw elephants, giraffes, and lots of monkeys. Today we saw lions! They were beautiful. I was a little bit scared, and I was happy when we got back to camp.

3 Read again and correct the sentences.
1. The Iguazu Falls are in Paraguay and Brazil.
2. Megan has tickets to visit the Louvre Museum in Paris.
3. Megan thought the elephants were beautiful but scary.

Today we landed in Sydney, Australia. We were very tired, but we were also very excited.

4 Write about one day on your around-the-world trip.

Speaking, Reading, and Writing 101

Think and Learn

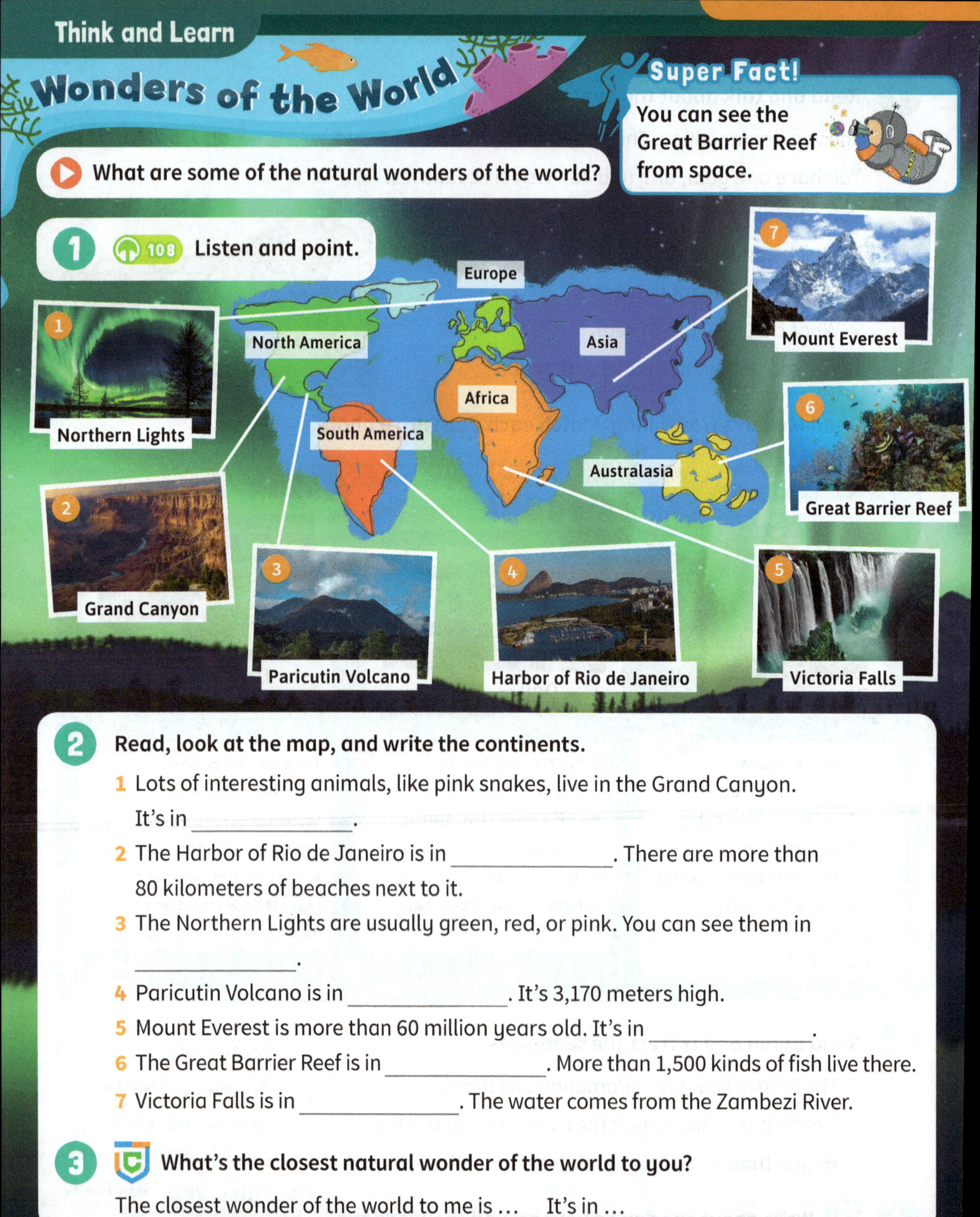

Wonders of the World

Super Fact! You can see the Great Barrier Reef from space.

▶ What are some of the natural wonders of the world?

1 🎧 108 Listen and point.

- 1 Northern Lights
- 2 Grand Canyon
- 3 Paricutin Volcano
- 4 Harbor of Rio de Janeiro
- 5 Victoria Falls
- 6 Great Barrier Reef
- 7 Mount Everest

Continents: Europe, North America, Asia, Africa, South America, Australasia

2 Read, look at the map, and write the continents.

1 Lots of interesting animals, like pink snakes, live in the Grand Canyon. It's in _____.

2 The Harbor of Rio de Janeiro is in _____. There are more than 80 kilometers of beaches next to it.

3 The Northern Lights are usually green, red, or pink. You can see them in _____.

4 Paricutin Volcano is in _____. It's 3,170 meters high.

5 Mount Everest is more than 60 million years old. It's in _____.

6 The Great Barrier Reef is in _____. More than 1,500 kinds of fish live there.

7 Victoria Falls is in _____. The water comes from the Zambezi River.

3 What's the closest natural wonder of the world to you?

The closest wonder of the world to me is … It's in …

Geography

4 🎧 109 **Match the facts with the man-made wonders. Listen and check.**

There are also wonders of the world made by people. We can call them "man-made" wonders. Here are some of them.

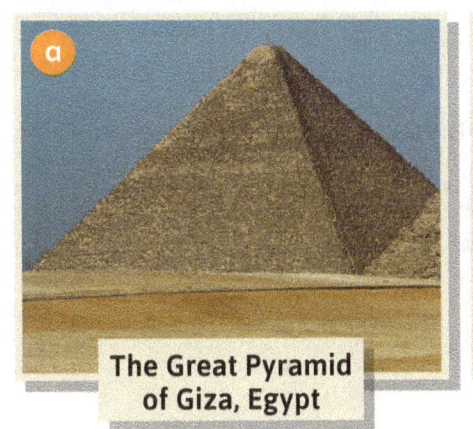

a) **The Great Pyramid of Giza, Egypt**
b) **The Great Wall, China**
c) **The Taj Mahal, India**

1. There are more than 2.3 million stones in it. ☐
2. The Emperor Shah Jahan built it to remember his wife. ☐
3. Many people think you can see it from the moon, but that's not true. ☐
4. It's 170 meters tall. ☐
5. They built it in 20 years. ☐
6. It's the longest wall in the world. ☐

5 **Talk about a natural or man-made wonder of the world. Use the words to help you.**

beautiful   old   big   interesting

> Which wonder of the world do you want to see?

> I want to see the Great Barrier Reef. It's very beautiful and very big.

6 ⭐ **Project** **Make a poster with your two favorite wonders of the world. Write a few sentences and a question about each wonder.**

My Favorite Wonders of the World

This is the Great Pyramid of Giza. It is in Egypt. How tall is it?

This is the Paricutin Volcano. It is the youngest volcano in America. How old is it?

Portfolio

Talk and Find Out

What Did We Do on Our Vacations?

1 **Make a prediction.**

I predict that _____ classmates visited the beach on vacation.

2 **Ask questions.**

What did you do on vacation?
- Visit relatives?
- Go to the beach?
- Go to the mountains?
- Visit a museum?
- Go camping?
- Go hiking?
- Relax?

3 **Write the information on the board.**

visit relatives – 6
go to the beach – 9
go to the mountains – 0

4 **Make a chart and talk about the results.**

> Was your prediction correct?

> Yes, it was. 9 classmates visited the beach on vacation.

WHAT WE DID

(bar chart: number of students by activity — relatives, beach, mountains, museum, camping, hiking, relax)

Communication

Think and Write

Write About a Country

1 Choose a country. Find information about the country. Make notes.

> Country: Spain
> Where: Europe
> Cities: Madrid, Barcelona, Málaga
> Famous for: ocean, mountains, sun, Picasso, soccer

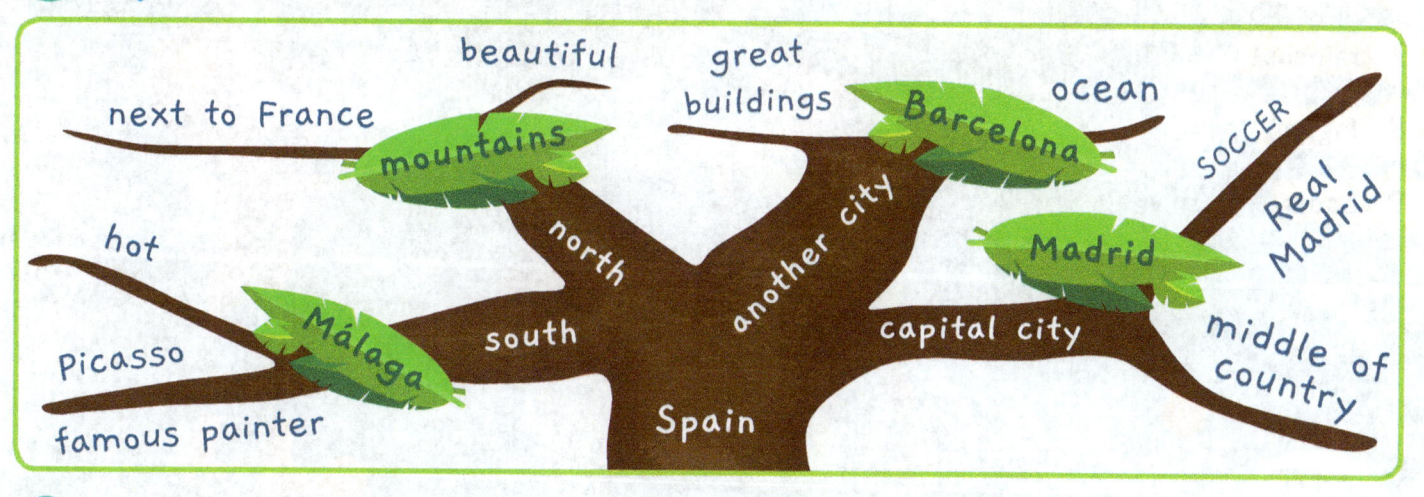

Writing Tip
Remember that names of cities and countries always start with a capital letter.

2 Make an information tree about your country.

Information tree for Spain:
- mountains: beautiful, next to France
- Barcelona: great buildings, ocean
- Madrid: SOCCER, Real Madrid, capital city, middle of country
- Málaga: hot, Picasso, famous painter, south
- north
- another city
- Spain

3 Find pictures and write about your country.

Spain is in Europe. The capital city is Madrid. It is in the middle of the country. Spain has two great soccer teams: Real Madrid and Barcelona. Barcelona is another famous city in Spain. It's by the ocean. It has lots of amazing buildings. There are beautiful mountains in the north of Spain, next to France. Picasso was a famous painter from Spain. One day, I would like to go to Spain for a vacation.

Writing 105

9 Vacation Plans

1 🎧 110 Listen and say the words. Then check with a friend.

1. thunderstorm
2. cloud(y)
3. lightning
4. rain(y)
5. wind(y)
6. umbrella
7. raincoat
8. fog(gy)
9. boots

BIG QUESTION How are vacations different?

2 🎧 111 Listen and correct the sentences.

1. Ben is scared of thunderstorms.
2. They are a long way from the castle.
3. Ben and Lucy have the book.
4. Ben and Lucy have to find two more letters.

3 Play the mime game.

I think you're holding an umbrella.

Yes, I am!

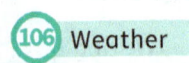

Weather

1 🎧 112 Listen and draw lines.

Monday **Tuesday** **Wednesday** **Thursday** **Friday**

sunny    foggy    rainy    cloudy    windy

2 Where do the words go? Say the sentences.

1 I'm be in the yard all day. (going to)
2 It's not going rainy on Tuesday. (to be)

3 ▶ 🎧 113 Watch, listen, and say.

Language Focus

It's **not going to be** sunny on Monday.
It's **not going to be** sunny on Wednesday.
And it's **going to be** rainy on Saturday.

Well, I'm **going to play** outside every day!
Do you want to come out, too?
Yes, I do! I'm **going to play** with you.

4 Play the weather game.

What's the weather going to be like tomorrow?

It's going to be foggy. I'm not going to play soccer.

Future with *be going to* + Infinitive

1 🎧 114 ▶ Listen and number the pictures. Then sing the song.

Vacation!
Enjoy your time away!
Vacation!
Let's shout Hooray! Hooray!

I'm going to stay in bed
And read my favorite book.
I'm going to see my aunt.
She's going to teach me how to cook.

Vacation! ...

I'm going to travel far away.
I'm going to have some fun.
Then I'm going to rest at home
And lie down in the sun.

Vacation! ...

After our vacation, we're going to be at school.
We're going to see our friends again.
Being with friends is cool!

Vacation! ...

2 Talk about your vacation.

> I'm going to read my favorite book.

3 Draw a Venn diagram.

> I'm not going to visit my aunt.

On vacation, I ...
get up late

call my grandma

On normal days, I ...
get up early

108 Singing for Pleasure

1 🎧 116 Listen, read, and write the names under the pictures.

1	2	3	4
_____	_____	_____	_____

Mrs. Beal: Lily, what are you going to do on your vacation?
Lily: Nothing much. I'm going to read lots of books.
Mrs. Beal: Oliver and James, what are you going to do?
James: We're going to stay home and play all our computer games.
Mrs. Beal: Ruby, what are you going to do on your vacation?
Ruby: I'm going to Mexico with my mom and dad. I'm going to swim all day.
Mrs. Beal: Dylan, what are you going to do on your vacation?
Dylan: I'm going to play lots of soccer and tennis.

2 Use the words to make *be going to* questions. Say the sentences.

1 Tim / what / you / do on your vacation?
2 Mom / what / we / do on our vacation?

3 ▶ 🎧 117 Watch, listen, and say.

Language Focus

Are you **going to climb** some trees?
Yes, I am.

Are you **going to eat** some candy?
No, I'm not.

Are you **going to go** away?
No, I'm not. I'm going to stay.

4 Look and play the vacation game.

Are you going to listen to music? Yes, I am.

Questions and Answers with *be going to* + Infinitive

The Treasure

1 🎧 118 ▶ Where are Ben and Lucy going to take the golden statue?

1
Lucy: Look. It's Horax and Zelda. What are they doing?
Ben: I don't know, but they have our book.
Lucy: Let's hide and find out.

2
Horax: There's a message with a missing word. We need the letters!
Ben: Achoo!
Zelda: What was that?

3
Horax: How kind of you to visit us!
Zelda: Now, give us the letters.
Ben: OK, they're N F D I S E R.
Horax: Hmm. So, it's a kind of puzzle.

4
Zelda: Go away, stupid dog!
Lucy: No! It can't be! You're Mr. Williams!
Horax: Yes, now you know. But it doesn't matter. I have what I need.

5
Horax: These letters are a puzzle.
Zelda: Yes. I think they make a word.
Horax: Look! The letters make the word *finders*. Let's write it!

6
Horax: What? The word has to be *finders*! That's what we are – finders!
Zelda: It's wrong, you fool. Why do you always get things wrong?

110 Reading for Pleasure

Lucy: The word is *friends* not *finders*. Only true friends can go in here. Come on, Ben!

Ben: Wow! It's beautiful!
Lucy: It's amazing! Let's take it to the museum. That's where it belongs.
Ben: What a perfect end to our adventure!

2 Use the code to find out what the statue says.

A B C D E F G H I J K L M N O P Q R S T U V W X Y Z

Phonics

3 Find who says … What a p**er**fect end to our adventure!

4 🎧 119 Listen and say.

There are c**ir**cles of p**ur**ple b**ir**ds wearing their vacation sh**ir**ts.

Phonics Focus: /ɜr/

Skills / Storytime

1 Read the story quickly. Write the answers.
  1 Where did Liam and his family go on vacation?
  2 What was the weather like?
  3 Why was it a very different vacation?

2 🎧 120 Read and listen. Check your answers.

A Very Different Vacation

Liam was very excited. "We're going to Florida for two weeks. We're going to swim a lot, and we're going to see lots of beautiful fish. It's going to be fantastic!" he said. His mom and dad were excited about the vacation, too. "We can go for boat rides!" said Dad. "We can relax and have a lot of fun!" said Mom.

They arrived in Florida in the afternoon. The hotel was beautiful and close to the ocean. Their rooms had big windows. Liam loved looking at the ocean and the boats. "Tomorrow I'm going to swim in the ocean!" he said.

That evening, they sat on the balcony for more than an hour. It was dark, and there were lots of stars. They listened to the ocean. "This is going to be a great vacation," said Liam.

In the middle of the night, Liam woke up. "What's that noise?" he thought. He looked outside and saw a big thunderstorm. Liam felt a little scared. "We're OK here, Liam," said Dad. "But the weather isn't looking good. Let's turn on the TV."

"There's going to be a lot of rain in Florida for the next fourteen days," said the man on TV. "There are going to be thunderstorms with strong winds and lots of lightning. It's going to be much colder than normal, too."

Value: Changing Perceptions; Reading Skills

Liam looked at his dad. Then he looked at his mom. They were both quiet. "That can't be true! It's our vacation. We can't swim or see fish in the rain! It's going to be boring," Liam said.

"The most important thing is that we're on vacation," answered Mom. "We can have fun in our room. We can read, play games, and listen to music. We don't need sun to have a good time!"

Two weeks later, their vacation was finished. "I don't want to go home, Mom," Liam said. "We didn't go swimming or see any beautiful fish, and we didn't go on a boat ride. But it was a beautiful vacation!"

"I agree," Mom said. "Let's finish packing later. Let's play another game first!" Dad went to get their games box. "Hooray!" shouted Liam.

3 Put the story in order.

- [ ] Liam had a good time inside with his mom and dad.
- [ ] Liam woke up because of a noisy thunderstorm.
- [ ] Liam and his mom and dad went to Florida for a vacation.
- [ ] Liam loved his vacation so much he didn't want to go home.
- [ ] Liam's dad turned on the TV.
- [ ] The man on TV said, "There's going to be rain for fourteen days!"
- [ ] Liam didn't like that. "It's going to be boring!" he thought.

4 🛡 🔼 121 Listen to a summary of the story. Write the four differences.

In the summary, we have …

1 ____Italy____ instead of ____Florida____.
2 _____ instead of _____.
3 _____ instead of _____.
4 _____ instead of _____.

Think and Learn

VACATIONS IN THE PAST

Super Fact!
100 years ago, people didn't go on vacation by plane. They went by train or boat.

▶ How were beach vacations different 100 years ago?

1 🎧 122 Listen and point.

1. puppet show
2. steam train
3. crowded beach
4. swimming boots
5. donkey ride
6. picnic basket
7. ice cream cart

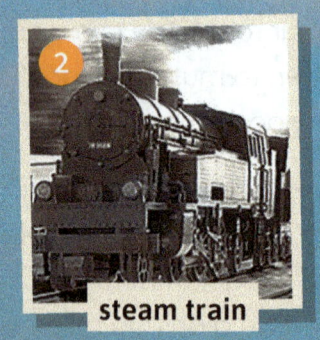

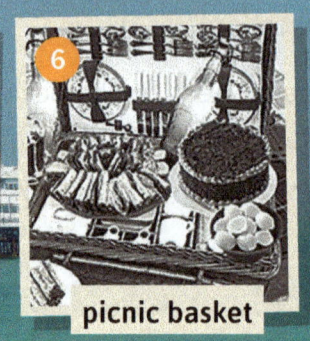

2 Read about beach vacations 100 years ago.

> 100 years ago, many families went on vacation to the beach by steam train. The beaches were very crowded with people. People wore special swimming boots in the water, but they didn't wear sunglasses. Children played in the sand and in the water. They liked watching puppet shows and going on donkey rides. Many families had picnic baskets with sandwiches, fruit, and lemonade in them for lunch. Sometimes, a cart came to the beach with ice cream for people to buy.

3 Match the sentences with the words.

1. This was crowded.
2. Many families went to the beach on this.
3. People went swimming in these.
4. Children liked watching this.
5. This had sandwiches in it.
6. Children liked riding this.
7. This sometimes came to the beach.

a an ice cream cart
b a picnic basket
c a donkey
d a steam train
e the beach
f a puppet show
g swimming boots

History

4 What's different about a beach vacation now and a beach vacation 100 years ago? Find two differences. Find two things that are the same.

> 100 years ago, people went to the beach by steam train. Now, they go by car.

5 Vacations now or vacations 50 years ago? Look at the pictures and write the numbers in the table.

Sleeping
1
2

Cooking
3
4

Playing
5 
6 

Camping 50 years ago	Camping now

6 Circle the pictures that you think could be in both groups.

7 **Project** Make a storyboard about a vacation when you were younger.

We went to the lake. We went by steam train.

We played with our ball and went swimming.

For lunch, we had a picnic and some ice cream.

We went for a long walk after lunch.

We felt happy.

History 115

Portfolio

Talk and Find Out

Vacation Time

1 Work in pairs. Read the role card.

You are going on vacation with a friend. Decide:
- Where you are going.
- How long you are going for.
- How you are going to get there.
- What you are going to do there.

Useful Language

Student A
I'd like to go to …
OK. What about … ?
We could …
Do you like … ?

Student B
I don't want to go to …
Yes, that's a great idea.
Fantastic!
Yes, I do. / No, I don't.

2 Plan your vacation.

I would like to go to Canada.

I don't want to go to Canada. How about the U.S.A.?

3 Work in groups.

Where are you going on vacation?

We are going to the U.S.A.

What are you going to do there?

We are going to go to Disney World. What about you?

Communication

Think and Write

Imagine a Vacation

1 Make a mind map about vacations.

- ON VACATION
  - good weather: go swimming, go snorkeling, watch TV
  - bad weather: read, play games, watch TV
  - places: by the ocean, in a city, on a mountain, in the country, play soccer
  - transportation: by plane, by bus, by car, by boat

2 Close your eyes for a minute. Imagine you are on vacation now. Write your ideas.

- Where are you? (at home / in another country)
- What was the weather like the last few days? (sunny / rainy / …)
- What did you do? (went snorkeling / read a book / …)
- What are you going to do in the next few days? (play games / …)

3 Write an email about your vacation.

Writing Tip
Use "Hi," "Hello," or "Dear" to start emails. Finish with "See you soon," "Love," or "Best wishes."

To: Anna@superminds.com
Subject: Hello from Wales!

Hello Anna,
We're on vacation in Wales. It's great. We're in a hotel by the ocean. The last few days, the weather wasn't good. It rained, but that wasn't a problem. We had lots of fun. We played games and read. In the evenings, we watched TV. The next few days are going to be better. We're going to swim in the ocean and play soccer on the beach. On Sunday, we're going to go hiking.
Love,
Trish

Language Focus: Meet the Explorers

Be good at + ing

I'm not **good at** rid**ing** bikes.
You're not **good at** snorkel**ing**.
He's/She's/It's **good at** play**ing** soccer.

Are you/they **good at** danc**ing**?
Is he/she **good at** play**ing** the piano?

He's/She's/It's not very **good at** cook**ing**.
We're **good at** climb**ing** trees.
They're not **good at** play**ing** tennis.

Yes, I/we/they **am**/**are**.
No, he/she **is**n't.

1 Complete the sentences.
1. I'm good at _____ a kite.
2. Our sister's not good at _____ horses.
3. My dad's not good at _____ breakfast.
4. They're good at _____ French.
5. We're not good at _____ puzzles.

It's not very good at cooking.

Possessive Apostrophe

Penny is Ben's sister.
Vivian is Jack's mom.
Ian's bike is red.

Paula's dog is very friendly.
Dad's car is very old.
My uncle's house is very big.

Paula's dog is very friendly.

2 Circle the correct word.
1. My **mom** / **mom's** is really nice.
2. My **mom** / **mom's** sister is my aunt.
3. **Brian** / **Brian's** bike is new.
4. **Brian** / **Brian's** is my friend.
5. I like **Sally** / **Sally's** cat.

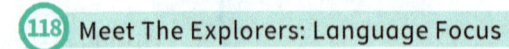

1 Our School

Like / Don't like + ing

I/You **like** writ**ing** stories.
He/She **loves** play**ing** computer games.
The dog **doesn't like** eat**ing** vegetables.

Do you/they **like** do**ing** homework?
Does he/she **like** sing**ing** in class?

We/They **love** go**ing** to the movie theater.
We/They **don't like** learn**ing** math.

Yes, I/we/they do.
No, he/she doesn't.

1 Circle the correct word.

1 Mike likes **play / playing** soccer.
2 I really don't like **walking / walk** to school.
3 They love **playing / play** computer games.
4 Do you like **cook / cooking**?

The dog doesn't like eating vegetables.

Have to / has to + Infinitive

Do you/they **have to go** to school on Saturdays?
Does he/she **have to make** breakfast in the morning?
I/You **have to do** homework every day.
Tom/Paula **has to wash** the dog every Sunday.
We/They **have to be** home before eight o'clock.

No, I/we/they don't.
Yes, he/she does.

2 Put the words in order.

1 have / wear / uniform / I / to / school

_____.

2 your / to / eat / have / you / beans

_____.

3 John / today / has / school / to / to / walk

_____.

Paula has to wash the dog every Sunday.

Unit 1: Language Focus 119

2 The Picnic

Questions and Answers with Some and Any

Is there **any** salad? Yes, there is **some** salad. / No, there isn't **any** salad.

Are there **any** grapes? Yes, there are **some** grapes. / No, there aren't **any** grapes.

1 Write *some* or *any*.

1 There aren't _____ parks in our town.
2 Are there _____ cookies in the cupboard?
3 There's _____ fish in this salad. Yuck!
4 There are _____ cats in the yard.
5 Is there _____ juice in the fridge?

Is there any salad?

No, there isn't any salad!

Suggestions

Should we **go** to the movie theater? Good idea!
Should we **dance**? No, thank you.
How about some sandwiches? OK.

Should we dance?

No, thank you!

2 Put the words in order.

1 soup / dinner / we / should / have / for
_____?

2 some / about / lemonade / how
_____?

3 cheese / lunch / how / a / for / about / sandwich
_____?

Unit 2: Language Focus

3 Daily Tasks

It's quarter to twelve, time for lunch!

Telling the Time

What time is it?

It's eleven **o'clock**.

It's **half past** eleven.

It's **quarter past** eleven.

It's **quarter to** twelve.

1 Look and complete the sentences.

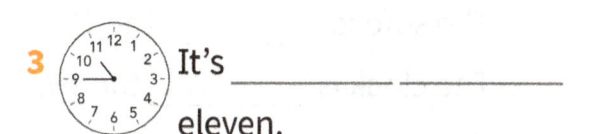

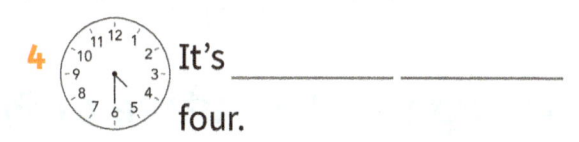

1. It's _____ _____ two.
2. It's _____ _____ seven.
3. It's _____ _____ eleven.
4. It's _____ _____ four.

Adverbs of Frequency

I **never** do homework on Saturdays.
He **sometimes** does the shopping.

We **usually** go to bed before eight o'clock.
They **always** say "please" and "thank you."

Do you **always** get up at seven o'clock? Yes, I **do**. / No, I **don't**.

2 Put the words in order.

1. mom / help / my / I / kitchen / always / the / in
   _____.

2. me / to / usually / Kevin / walks / school / with
   _____.

3. sometimes / dad / cooks / my / dinner
   _____.

He sometimes does the shopping.

Unit 3: Language Focus

4 Around Town

Prepositions

My house is **across from** the school.
The café's **near** the bank.
Where's your school?

The cat's **above** the TV.
My bag's **below** the stairs.
It's **near** the park.

The cat is above the TV.

1 Look and complete the sentences.

1 The sofa is _____ the painting.
2 The sofa is _____ the TV.
3 The clock is _____ the TV.
4 The baby is _____ the table.

Be going to + Infinitive of Purpose

Where are you/we/they going?
Where's he/she going?

I**'m**/We**'re**/They**'re going to** the store **to get** some milk.
He**'s**/She**'s going to** the flower store **to buy** some flowers.

I**'m**/You**'re**/We**'re**/They**'re going to** the pool **to go** swimming.
He**'s**/She**'s going to** the station **to take** a train.

I'm going to the pool to go swimming.

2 Complete the sentences.

1 I'm going to the _____ to play tennis.
2 She's going to the _____ to get a book.
3 We're going to the _____ to wait for a bus.
4 Dad's going to the _____ to get some money.
5 They're going to the _____ to see a movie.

5 Under the Ocean

Was / Were

I **was** really tired last night.
You **were** very angry.
He **was** my friend.
She **wasn't** very happy.

It **was** quiet in the classroom.
We **weren't** at school today.
They **were** very happy to see us.

1 Write *was* or *were*.

1. My grandfather _____ a teacher.
2. I _____ very sad.
3. My dad's first car _____ pink!
4. Yes, we _____ at the party.
5. Jim and Tony _____ scared of the octopus.

I was really tired last night.

Questions and Answers with *Was / Were*

Were you at school?
Was he/she at home?
Where **were** you?

Yes, I **was**.
Yes, he/she **was**.
I **was** at my aunt's house.

No, I **wasn't**.
No, he/she **wasn't**.

Were you at school?

2 Circle the correct word.

1. **Was / Were** the class difficult?
2. Where **was / were** the books?
3. **Was / Were** Nathan and Adam at the party?
4. Where **was / were** your mom's car keys?
5. **Was / Were** there a dolphin in the ocean?

Yes, I was.

Unit 5: Language Focus 123

6 Gadgets

Comparatives

My car is **faster than** yours.
Your shoes are **cleaner than** my shoes.
The blue cell phone is **more expensive than** the red one.

Math is **more difficult than** science.
Your ice cream cone is **bigger than** my ice cream cone!
I think Ben is **happier than** me today.

1 Use comparatives to complete the sentences.

1 Their car is _____ than our car. (expensive)
2 His scooter is _____ than my scooter. (big)
3 That yard is _____ than our yard. (beautiful)
4 My skateboard is _____ than your skateboard. (cheap)
5 Rachel is always _____ than her sister. (happy)

Your ice cream cone is bigger than my ice cream cone!

Superlatives

It's **the biggest** cat in the world.
He's **the happiest** person in my family.
This is **the cheapest** cell phone in the store.

The smallest park in the world is in the United States.
It's **the most exciting** movie ever!

2 Put the words in order.

1 class / in / our / I'm / smallest / the / boy
   _____.
2 beautiful / in / most / Africa / snake / the / it's
   _____.
3 it's / on / the / beach / the / sandcastle / biggest
   _____.
4 soccer player / most / the / world's / expensive / he's
   _____.

It's the biggest cat in the world.

7 In the Hospital

Simple Past: Regular Verbs

I/You play**ed** basketball yesterday.
She/He walk**ed** to school this morning.
The helicopter land**ed** on the building.
We/They watch**ed** TV after school.

1 Use the verbs in parentheses to talk about yesterday.

1. I _____ into the swimming pool. The water was very cold! (jump)
2. We _____ at his hat. (smile)
3. My sister _____ dinner last night. (cook)
4. My aunt _____ me with my homework yesterday. (help)
5. Ursula and Bridget _____ computer games in the afternoon. (play)

The helicopter landed on the building.

Simple Past: Irregular Verbs

I **felt** tired all day.
You **rode** a dinosaur! Really?
Mr. Linford **gave** me the wrong book.
She **went** to bed at eight o'clock.
It **said**, "Meow," I think.
We **had** a lot to eat at lunch.
They **woke up** at half past six.

2 Write the infinitives.

1. felt _____
2. gave _____
3. had _____
4. woke up _____
5. went _____
6. said _____

It said, "Meow," I think.

Unit 7: Language Focus 125

8 Around the World

Negatives with Simple Past

I **didn't play** ice hockey!
You **didn't eat** all your food.
He **didn't visit** his grandfather on Sunday.
She **didn't like** my present.

It **didn't snow** last night.
We **didn't go** to school today.
They **didn't want** to help me.

1 Complete the sentences.

1. They went to England, but they _____ to London.
2. She gave me a present, but she _____ one to my sister.
3. We had math today, but we _____ history.
4. I felt sick last night, but I _____ sick this morning.
5. He had some sandwiches, but he _____ any lemonade.

She didn't like my present.

Questions and Answers with Simple Past

Did you **have** fun at the party?
Did he/she **say**, "Thank you"?
Did we/they **do** something wrong?
When **did** you **see** Juan?
Where **did** you **see** him?

Yes, I **did**.
No, he **didn't**.
Yes, you **did**.
Yesterday.
At school.

Yes, she **did**.
No, they **didn't**.

Did you have fun at the party?

2 Complete the questions and answers.

1. _____ you do the shopping?   Yes, I _____.
2. _____ she find her cat?   No, she _____.
3. _____ they go by train?   No, they _____.
4. _____ we win?   No, we _____.
5. _____ he help you?   Yes, he _____.

Yes, I did.

126 Unit 8: Language Focus

9 Vacation Plans

Future with *be going to* + Infinitive

I**'m going to send** you a postcard.
You **aren't going to eat** that!
He**'s going to buy** a new raincoat.
She **isn't going to take** the bus today.

It**'s going to be** windy tomorrow.
We**'re going to play** tennis now.
They**'re going to learn** French.

1 Complete the sentences.

not rain   cook   build   call   not have

1 I'm _____ Lisa this evening.
2 It _____ this afternoon.
3 You're _____ dinner.
4 We _____ fish and chips for dinner.
5 Dad's _____ me a new tree house.

You aren't going to eat that!

Questions and Answers with *be going to* + Infinitive

Am I **going to get** better soon?
Are you **going to watch** TV on the weekend?
Is he/she **going to make** a cake for your birthday?
Are we/they **going to take** the bus?

Yes, you are.
Yes, I am.
Yes, he/she is.
No, we/they aren't.

Am I going to get better soon?

Yes, you are.

2 Use the verbs in parentheses to talk about the future.

1 Are you _____ your grandparents this weekend? (visit)
2 Is he _____ at your house tonight? (sleep)
3 Are your mom and dad _____ you with your school project? (help)
4 Is your sister _____ you a birthday present? (give)
5 Are we _____ pizza tonight? (have)

Unit 9: Language Focus 127